FLAMES OVER PERSEPOLIS

MORTIMER WHEELER

FLAMES OVER PERSEPOLIS

TURNING-POINT IN HISTORY

Reynal & Company, Inc.
in association with
William Morrow & Company, Inc., New York

REYNAL & COMPANY, INC.
in association with
William Morrow & Company, Inc., New York

Library of Congress Catalog No. 68–25488

Phototypeset in England by
BAS Printers Limited, Wallop, Hampshire

Printed in Italy

CONTENTS

FOREWORD

Of the Nine Worthies of medieval pageantry, some were liable to be changelings. Fashion or fantasy might drop Godfrey de Bouillon for Guy of Warwick, or Shakespeare might enlist Pompey and Hercules who have no place in Caxton's catalogue. But Alexander the Great was infallible. I remember long ago seeing the painted figures of the Nine brought to light on the tattered plaster of a Tudor house at Amersham in Buckinghamshire: Julius Caesar with a tilting lance, and headgear for all the world like a plumed bowler-hat; Duke Joshua with sword and lance and scarlet caparison; and a bearded ruffian, some local rustic, in classical armour of a Renaissance kind, whom we hailed as Alexander himself – the name had gone to dust . . . In the depths of the British Museum a Harleian MS. (2259) of the fifteenth century declares his arms: *goules a lyon gold, soyaunt in a cheyre syluer, enbatellyd with a pollax sabill.* He was near to the heart of the Middle Ages, as of all Ages, past and to come.

Perhaps that is why, when my Publishers invited me to write a little book for general reading based upon some historic episode of my choice, my mind turned immediately to this most human of all heroes, complete with his golden lion and his sable pole-axe. When, more than twenty years since, I found myself for the first time amidst the upstanding pillars of the palace of the Persian King of Kings at Persepolis, the thought of just such a book entered my head; and since then other circumstances have converged upon the notion. At Persepolis I stood and looked upon the stones where Alexander had indeed sat upon a 'cheyre' that may well enough have been of gold and silver. Here in fact, within this very building, he was midway in his great adventure, both in time and place. Here was the hinge of his whole enterprise. Had he turned back here, his followers – or some of them – would have applauded, but the history of the humanities would have been impoverished beyond estimate. As it was, from Persepolis he swept across central Asia like a jungle-fire, and all manner of new and civilized things grew amidst the ashes. From Persepolis to the Punjab let it be his proud epitaph: Alexander passed this way.

And yet it is astonishing how very little actual trace we have of his passing. Vivid though his historical literature be and flaming his Romance, his material presence has evaded us. It is almost as though a disembodied idea had come and gone as a mighty spiritual force with little immediate tangibility. We know more, in material terms, of Agamemnon than of Alexander. We plod as camp-followers in the train of Julius Caesar, but Bucephalus outpaces us. This is an embarrassment and at the same time a healthy stimulus to the materially minded archaeologist, and it is a function of this book to show summarily how he is facing up to the challenge.

Alexander the Great. What did he look like? Of that at least, we have an inkling. Copies of the sculptured portraits of him by the great Lysippus and his peers have survived and are convincing (frontispiece). They show his full and youthful face set aslant (by habit or by some trifling deformity) upon a sturdy neck; the chin is heavy and rounded, the mouth small, the eyes deep-set with the slightly upward glance which was characteristic of his era, perhaps because he moulded it; the turbulent hair streams towards his shoulders, in the manner of the modern *avant-garde*. The whole aspect is one of mingled determination, intelligence and abandon. It is Alexander.

But when we turn to his works upon the vast landscape which he traversed, there is, it is true, pitifully little as yet to see. His exploits lay, more often than not, in regions difficult of access. With acceptable likelihood the redoubtable Aurel Stein identified the scene of the conqueror's assault upon the Rock of Aornos, in the mountains adjacent to the Indian frontier, and a vivid reconstruction of the episode can be attempted on the ground by those hardy enough to follow Stein's (and Alexander's) footsteps. For the rest there are now at last signs of accelerated discovery. The other day, directly aided by the Afghan King, my friends of the French Archaeological Delegation which has worked in Afghanistan since 1922 achieved one of their ancient ambitions by finding the site of a Hellenistic city on the banks of the Oxus, and have begun to dig there. It is expected to be one of Alexander's own Alexandrias, and the expectation may well be realized before these words are published. Meanwhile on later pages I have been able to say something about the site and its possibilities. The new evidence from this, the first of the foundations of the Greeks in Bactria to be submitted to effective excavation, may easily be revolutionary.

Of another kind was a small but gratifying discovery which came my way at the ancient Pushkalavati, capital of Gandhara, when I was trying out the site in 1958. This discovery was (as I claim it) that of the defensive rampart and ditch built round the city on the approach of Alexander's troops in 327 BC. Thereafter it took the invaders a month to capture the place, so the rampart and its garrison may be thought to have deserved this small and earthy memento of their prowess. More will be said of the episode in its proper context.

But all this is short-term stuff, as yet of little moment though full of promise. At present it is to the long-term sequel of the conqueror's transit that we may turn with greater satisfaction. And it is this long-term sequel that lends to the whole Alexander-episode both an endurance and a diversity that are alike amazing and without comparison. In a few months the hero had charged across the Afghan highlands and the Punjab plains. He left behind him cities of his own foundation where, generations after his passing, good Hellenistic Greek was still, as recent discoveries have shown, used alike for the repetition of old Delphic wisdom and of new Indian humanism. His Greek and no doubt half-Greek successors in these remote regions left their stamp upon some of the finest coinage that Hellenistic moneyers – or any others – ever wrought. Nor was all this Hellenism merely the dwindling preserve of a few Greek expatriates or their Hellenizing dependants. Wave after wave of nomads from inner Asia moved down upon the scene and fell into line with Hellenistic thinking; learned to ape the Greek fashion in urban planning, and clung with varying skill to Greek artistry. And the greatest of these Asian peoples, four centuries or more after Alexander, in turn picked the bones of all this Hellenism, recarved the Greek alphabet to fit their own Iranian tongue, and became the patrons of a new composite art in which, reinvigorated and supplemented from various sources, some element of the old Hellenism still lived on.

At the same time a parallel sequel to Persepolis and its aftermath had, more quietly but with even longer consequence, been making itself perceptible far across the Indian plains and deep into the midst of the subcontinent. This was the dispersal, the *diaspora*, of Persian craftsmanship and its partial re-establishment in the successor-empire of the Indian Mauryas, where it was destined to evolve in collaboration some of the basic and most enduring features of Indian architecture. Whether this formative influence from Persia would have found its way somehow into India in circumstances other than those created by Alexander is an idle guess; at most it was an unintended by-product of his errantry. Let it simply be ascribed to his uncanny aptness for happy coincidence, that he appeared impulsively upon the scene at the precise moment when a subcontinent, lacking any established architectural tradition of its own, was politically ascendant and culturally in receptive mood. Achaemenian Persepolis was a blackened ruin, but Mauryan Pataliputra rose in its stead.

Briefly, from Persepolis to the twelve terminal altars which, maybe, still await discovery beside the river Beas in the Punjab, the Alexander Adventure assumed a cosmic quality that is unsurpassed – unrivalled – in the whole story of human endeavour. As far as Persepolis the Macedonian had been manoeuvring within the framework of ancient and evolved civilizations. He was a conqueror, ambitious and brilliantly successful but not uniquely creative. Eastward of Persepolis, in the outlands of Asia, he achieved a more exalted and lasting destiny. Himself a highly Hellenized 'barbarian' or non-Greek, he was now with increasing awareness, it would seem, the pioneer of a new concept of civilization, based not upon the conventional dichotomy of Greek and non-Greek but upon a universal *homonoia* or equality of status and understanding. Diodorus the Sicilian, compiling in the first century BC and supported perhaps by implication in passages of Strabo, Plutarch and Arrian, cites a 'memorandum' by Alexander which professes to show that he was beginning to think in international terms far in advance of his epoch. Whether literally historical or not, the memorandum has a certain ring of truth about it: he was planning, we are told, to create 'cities with mixed populations, to transplant peoples from Asia to Europe [i.e. Greece] and in the opposite direction from Europe to Asia, and so to establish the greatest continents in common unity and friendly kinship by intermarriages and domestic ties'. On such showing, it can be claimed for him (and was so claimed by Tarn) that he was the first true internationalist. The evidence falls short of proof; but, whether it be accepted or not, a steady accumulation of material data in recent years is valid witness to the new integration of East and West that ensued from his intelligent adventuring. Summaries of this new material are included in the following pages.

In all the circumstances it is fair to affirm that the burning of Persepolis marked a major divide, not merely in the particular history and archaeology of Eurasia, but in the broad history and archaeology of ideas.

1967   M.W.

THE
BURNING

Autumn was fading into winter of the year 331 BC when Alexander the Great, now at the ripe age of twenty-five, came to Persepolis, a capital city and palace of the Persian King of Kings. His mood, we are told, was one of violence and distrust. His miscellaneous army was far from home in a testing environment of alternating indulgence and privation. His principal enemy had escaped into difficult and distant hill-country and was there preparing new hazards for him. The logistics of supply, recruitment and relief would alone have baffled a less buoyant intelligence; hints in the histories show that they were ever present to his mind. And on the road to Persepolis a human episode had stirred his ready passion beyond the ordinary.

He had bridged the river Araxes and entered the province of Persis, whereof Persepolis was the chief city, when he was confronted with a strange and terrible spectacle. In his path stood a motley crowd of some eight hundred men, mostly of advanced age, bearing branches in token of respect and supplication. It turned out that they were Greeks who had been dragged or enticed from their homes in the West by former kings of Persia as skilled craftsmen or knowledgeable apprentices. There was nothing very notable about this: a century and a half previously, Greek artists had already been employed at Persepolis and in their spare time had scratched bearded heads of about 500–490 BC on the polished stone shoe of a sculptured figure of Darius (see above); and long afterwards, in Roman times,

Greek technicians – Yavanas or Ionians – were widely employed in the Orient. But what shocked Alexander and brought tears to his eyes was the sorry condition of those who now approached him. All of them had been mutilated in macabre and systematic fashion, by the removal of those extremities which were not needed individually for their specific occupations. Some had lost their hands, some their feet, some their ears and noses, escape thus being rendered impossible or undesirable.

With one voice these unhappy *mutilés* besought Alexander's aid; and he, having summoned their leaders and received them with the sympathy and respect characteristic of him, promised to do all in his power to restore them to their Greek homes. Thereupon they gathered together and took counsel, but in the upshot decided to stay there rather than to return home. 'If they were brought back to safety, they would be scattered in small numbers, and as they settled amongst their cities they would suffer contumely for their misfortunes. But if they continued to live together in their common plight they would have the consolation of sharing their misery with their fellows in like condition. So they repaired again to the king and told him of their decision, asking him for help appropriate to this proposal.' Alexander (no doubt with considerable relief) applauded the decision, and gave each of them 3,000 drachmae, five men's robes and the same number for women, two yoke of oxen, fifty sheep, and fifty measures of wheat. He also exempted them from all royal taxes, and ordered his officials to see that they were wronged by no one.

[This pitiful story is recounted by Diodorus Siculus, Curtius, and Justin.]

The incident can have done nothing to mitigate Alexander's own description of Persepolis as 'the most hateful of the cities of Asia'. Save for the royal palace, he gave it over to his troops, and for a whole day his Macedonians plundered it without satisfying their greed for more. 'It was the richest city under the sun, and the private houses had been filled with every sort of comfort over many years. The Macedonians rushed in to the slaughter of all men and plundered their properties, many of them belonging to the ordinary citizens but full of furniture and fine equipment. Here abundant silver was carried off, and not a little gold and much costly raiment, some with sea-purple and some with gold embroidery – all this became the prize of the victors. The great and world-famed palaces fell to despicable and utter ruination.'

But not the greatest palace of them all. Whilst still on the march Alexander had received from the Great King's agent at the royal palace (his name is preserved to us – one Tiridates) a message to the effect that if the king could anticipate the arrival of Persian reinforcements he would be admitted without resistance. Now, whilst the nearby city was the noisy scene of every sort of violence, Alexander mounted the great stairways to the terrace upon which the mighty colonnaded halls stood, and still in no

mean measure stand (pages 8–9). It may be that Tiridates was there to receive and guide him; one compiler (Curtius) records that Tiridates was rewarded, and this would have been the appropriate moment. An older account (that of Diodorus) briefly informs us that 'Alexander took possession of the Treasures there', and the reputable Arrian says much the same. These treasures had accumulated since the time of the first Persian king, Cyrus, and the storerooms were full of gold and silver to the amount of 120,000 talents. Keeping some of this for the current expenses of the campaign, he sent to Babylon and Mesopotamia and Susa for a great number of mules, both for packs and for harness, together with 3,000 pack camels, to transport the rest to Susa. In one way and another, he was clearing Persepolis of all its valuables, as though in preparation for its destined fate. 'He vehemently detested the inhabitants', says Diodorus, 'and hastened Persepolis towards its final end.'

But by this time winter was upon him. In these parts the weather from December to March is liable to range from torrential rain to considerable falls of snow: no season for major campaigning. During the four months Alexander rested and no doubt re-trained his satiated troops, whilst incidentally disposing of his treasures. It was not in his nature to be idle. We may see him hunting in the hills round about Persepolis, striving by

PERSEPOLIS: *entrance to the 'Throne Hall' of Xerxes, with relief showing the seated King and attendant*

precept and example to preserve his officers from the lures of oriental comfort, with its accompanying temptations to intrigue and disruption; exploring Persis, and accepting or exacting homage; sitting anon in state, no doubt with an exuberant sense of theatre, beneath the golden canopy of the throne of the King of Kings amidst the hundred columns of the palatial throne-room; and generally usurping the habitude of a great oriental monarch, tempered by the virility of a Western upbringing and the urgency of a restless mind.

The advent of spring in 330 BC meant the resumption of large-scale action. It meant first and foremost the final pursuit of the refugee King of Kings himself. The third Darius was reported to be on his way, with 30,000 Persians and Greek mercenaries, to the province of Bactria, beside the river Oxus in what is nowadays known as Afghan Turkestan. There he hoped to reassemble his uncertain forces in some sort of fighting shape, though he himself had little enough of fighting spirit in him. The end was near. It was anticipated by a lurid incident which lit a beacon in the history of Asia.

The four surviving historians of Alexander's progress tell of the incident, though with differing emphasis. All of them wrote between the first century BC and the second century AD but derived their information ultimately from the record left by Alexander's own companions, and the central facts, however trimmed with fantasy, are beyond dispute. Before the invaders left Persepolis, the great palace was put to the flames; and, twenty-two centuries later, archaeologists digging amidst the ruins found widespread evidence of the burning. Thus 'the entire floor of the main hall was covered with a layer of ashes and charcoal, which on microscopic analysis proved to be cedar; that is, carbonized remains of roof beams. Herzfeld states that this layer was from one foot to three feet thick, and he describes the effect of fire upon the column remnants. . . . There is no doubt that the collapse of the Throne Hall and its portico was caused by a conflagration, which may well have coincided with the burning of the Treasury, situated beyond the street to the south, and perhaps with the destruction of the Apadana itself', that is, of the columned audience-hall to the west of the Throne Room. References to all this and other evidences of the kind are collected in Erich Schmidt's large volume on *Persepolis*, published in 1953 by the University of Chicago Press.

Of the accounts of the episode itself, that of Arrian, an Asiatic Greek who served the emperor Hadrian and died about AD 180, smacks typically of the deep freeze and is historically free from contamination. Alexander, says Arrian, burnt the palace of the Persian kings, though against the advice of his trusted Parmenio 'who urged him to spare it for various reasons, chiefly because it was hardly wise to destroy what was his own property, and because the Asians would, in his opinion, be less willing to

opposite
PERSEPOLIS:
eastern stairway to the Hall of Audience. A stallion brought as tribute to the Great King. Time of Xerxes

support him if he seemed bent merely upon passing through their country as a conqueror rather than upon ruling it securely as a king. Alexander's answer was that he wished to punish the Persians for their invasion of Greece; his present act was retribution for the destruction of Athens, the burning of the temples, and all the other crimes that they had committed against the Greeks. My own view is that this was bad policy; moreover it could hardly be considered as punishment for Persians long since dead and gone.'

On this showing, the burning of Persepolis in 330 BC was a cold and deliberate act of vengeance for the burning of the Athenian Acropolis and the towns and temples of Attica by Xerxes in 480 BC. And so no doubt in essence it was. Alexander's invasion of Persian Asia had from the outset partaken, if only for propaganda purposes, of a crusade of vengeance against the descendants of those who had wrought so much wrong to Greece a hundred and fifty years before. This was made sufficiently clear to the Persian king in 333 BC when, after the Macedonian victory at the Issus in the borderland between Cilicia and Syria, Alexander replied defiantly to an appeal from Darius with the opening words: 'Your ancestors invaded Macedonia and Greece and caused havoc in our country, though we had done nothing to provoke them. As supreme commander of all Greece I invaded Asia because I wished to punish Persia for this act . . .' (Arrian).

But Arrian's bleak mention of the destruction of the palace as an act of punitive policy is not perhaps the whole story. From Diodorus Siculus, compiling in the latter half of the first century BC, to Dryden's *Alexander's Feast*, written for St Cecilia's festival in 1697, the episode was liable to be tricked out in the fashion of grand opera rather than of history. Let us begin with Diodorus (XVII, 72).

It was the farewell party in the palace. 'When the company was full of good cheer and the drinking was far advanced, drunkenness began to prevail and frenzy possessed the minds of the drinkers. Then one of the women present, Thaïs by name and Attic by race, said that for Alexander it would be his finest deed in Asia if he joined with them in a triumphal procession, set fire to the palace, and let the hands of women make short shrift of the glories of the Persians. These words being said to young men naturally elevated by wine beyond all reason, someone shouted to lead on and snatch up torches, and exhorted all to revenge the outrages against the temples of the Greeks. And others taking up the cry and saying that this deed was worthy of Alexander alone, the king took fire at their words, and all leapt up from their drinking and passed word for the marshalling of a procession in honour of Dionysus.

'Quickly numbers of flares were collected. Many women-musicians were present at the party, and the king led them out in procession with song and flutes and pipes, with Thaïs the courtesan at the head of the performance. And she, after the king, was the first to hurl her blazing torch into the palace. The others did the same, so that swiftly the whole region of the palace was consumed with fire owing to the magnitude of the conflagration. And it was the greatest of paradoxes that the impious act of Xerxes, king of the Persians, against the Acropolis of the Athenians was repaid in kind, many years afterwards and in sport, by one woman, a fellow-citizen of those who had suffered.'

More than a century after Diodorus, Plutarch transcribed the sources in a generally similar fashion that nevertheless bears repetition. 'On the point of marching out against Darius, it happened that he [Alexander] consented to take part with his companions in a merry drinking-party in which women also drank and shared in the rout with their lovers. Most popular amongst these women was Thaïs, who came from Attica and was the mistress of Ptolemy who later became king. She, partly to flatter and partly to amuse Alexander, as the drinking proceeded was moved to address him in a manner suitable to the character of her native country though in a more ostentatious fashion than was fitting for her. For she said that all the hardships she had endured in her wanderings through Asia had been rewarded that day by revelling in the splendid palace of the Persians; but it would be a still sweeter thing to go in a rout and set fire to the house of that Xerxes who had burnt Athens, she herself kindling the flames under the

PERSEPOLIS:
eastern stairway to the
Hall of Audience.
A Bactrian camel
brought as tribute

eyes of the king so that word might go out to all peoples that the women in the following of Alexander wrought a greater punishment upon the Persians in the name of Hellas than did her admirals and generals put together. At these words there was loud applause and eager encouragement and emulation amongst the company. The king was persuaded and, leaping to his feet, led the way with a garland on his head and a torch in his hand. The rest, following in rout and uproar, flocked round the palace; the other Macedonians, hearing about it, joyfully joined the party with torches. For they hoped that the burning and destruction of the palace meant that the thought was now of home and that there was no intention of remaining amongst foreigners. Thus spontaneously some say that the deed was done; others believe that it was all an act of premeditation. But it is agreed that Alexander changed his mind and ordered that the fire be extinguished.' As we have seen, archaeology shows that if he did so he was too late.

These are the two principal accounts, those of Diodorus and Plutarch. Between them apparently comes Curtius, whose account is similar to that of Diodorus and may have been derived from it. Of the two quoted, from the literary standpoint there is no doubt that, in the Greek, Plutarch's version is the more vivid and eloquent. Plutarch was an artist, Diodorus in comparison a mere compiler. But, artistry apart, a fundamental question arises: what is the historical value of this picturesque tradition? Is it true?

The admirable Sir William Tarn would have none of it. 'I need hardly say that there is not a word of truth in the Thaïs story. Alexander burnt Xerxes's palace deliberately, as a political manifesto to Asia. . . . Alexander habitually dined with his generals, but to suppose that he dined their mistresses too would be merely silly[?] . . . As to the crowd of flute-girls and such, it *was* a Greek custom to have flute-girls in after dinner, but it was not a Macedonian custom, apart from the fact that such a practice would have been entirely out of keeping with Alexander's character[??]. These girls belong to the circle of ideas which made him perpetually drunken. . . . Aristobulus, who knew far more about Alexander than any popular writer did, said that he sat long at dinner, but for the sake of friendly conversation, not of wine; that alone suffices to negative the flute-girls[???] . . .' And so forth. Well, well. If one thing is more certain than another, it is that, at least in the latter part of his career, Alexander would swill his wine with the next man. The reputable sources used by Appian are not in doubt about this. At the time of his murder of the offensive Cleitus there had been 'some pretty heavy drinking', and in drink Alexander himself 'now tended to barbaric excess'. On this occasion 'he showed himself the slave of anger and drunkenness' and 'his wits were fuddled with wine'. On another occasion he 'sat up drinking until dawn', thus, unknown to him, frustrating the murderous plot of the young squires. But this did not prevent the ringleader at his trial from accusing Alexander of 'heavy drinking' and 'drunken sleep'; and it is to be presumed that the accusation had some verisimilitude. It may be feared that Sir William Tarn, from his twentieth-century Scottish retreat, had had no great experience of campaigning at the age of twenty-six far from home, amidst the outlands of an alien continent in the fourth century BC. With all his acute scholarship, for interpreting the Hellenistic period he had, as the perspicacious Rostovtzeff remarked, one disadvantage: he was 'dominated by the instincts of an English gentleman'.

Hero-worship apart, what are the historical facts of the incident? The basic surviving fact is this: Cleitarchus of Alexandria published a work about Alexander at a date subsequent, but probably not long subsequent, to 282 BC, i.e. not much more than forty-one years after Alexander's death. He did not indeed accompany Alexander; the supposition would not strain chronology beyond tolerance, but other possible reasons have been adduced. He wrote nevertheless at a time when there were still survivors of Alexander's campaigns and in a country (Egypt) which was until 282 ruled by one of Alexander's principal generals and first-hand historians, Ptolemy I. (He may well have written considerably before King Ptolemy's death in 282 and have withheld publication on the delicate ground that Thaïs was Ptolemy's mistress.) True, Cleitarchus had no very savoury reputation amongst later writers; Strabo, for example, at the end of the first century BC, speaks of his 'many lies', and in the following century Quintilian described him as 'able but untrustworthy'. Nevertheless, it is difficult to imagine that, in describing a key-episode such as the burning of Persepolis, he should have invented a highly circumstantial chain of events which could be checked by living memory. And what does he say? In one of the thirty-six meagre fragments of his work which have survived, he is quoted (by that inveterate collector, Athenaeus) as asserting that 'Thaïs was the cause of the burning of the palace at Persepolis'. Is not that enough to make Thaïs (historically) a believable if not particularly respectable character? And with Thaïs as the accepted cause, the remainder of the episode follows. There is, it seems to me, no justification whatsoever for rejecting the Thaïs episode more or less in the shape which Diodorus, Curtius and Plutarch have bequeathed to us. That Arrian omits the details has no bearing upon the matter; a businesslike and even arid brevity was his habit. And as to Tarn, I am prepared in this context to reinforce Rostovtzeff's observation with Sir Frank Adcock's parallel comment that 'Tarn's judgment might, now and then, be deflected by the application of standards too traditionally ethical for the times of which he wrote'. No, the romantic fifteenth-century poetaster (British Museum Harleian MSS. 2259, folio 39 verso) was not altogether wide of the mark when he wrote

> Lo, alexander, that wan ner all erthe,
> Yett have wyne and women hym conqueryd.

Let us then accept the likelihood that the last party in Xerxes's palace was a good one, and that at its climax the retrospect of Xerxes himself amidst the smoking ruins of Attica was an excusably irritant memory. The touch added by Plutarch – the nostalgic hope on the part of some of those present that the burning would mark the ultimate limit of the Asian enterprise – fits likewise into the picture. And so, *pace* Tarn, does the impulsive Thaïs.

Thence onwards, only the headlong impetus of Alexander held his reluctant army on its eastward course. Thither we need not follow it in detail, full of incident though it was. Suffice it that Darius was betrayed and murdered by his own Bactrian satrap. Alexander, riding hard so that only sixty of his followers kept up with him, came upon the Persian cortège at the moment when Darius was on the point of death. As they galloped in, the horses of the Macedonians trod gold and silver vessels under their hooves amid panic-stricken wagonloads of women and children. With difficulty, Alexander found the Persian king lying in a wagon, nearing the end, his body full of javelins (see above). The dying man asked for drink, and putting to his lips some cold water said to Polystratos who had given it to him, 'My man, this is the uttermost limit of my ill-fortune, that I have received kindness and cannot return it. But Alexander will reward you for your kindness, and the gods will reward Alexander for his own kindness to my [captured] mother, wife and children. To him, through you, I give this right hand.' So saying, and taking the hand of Polystratos, he died. A gracious episode, whether veracious or contrived; and, even if contrived, no doubt essentially true to the spirit alike of the generous Macedonian and of the unhappy oriental aristocrat, to whom good dying was a natural part of good breeding. To complete the story, when Alexander came up he was manifestly affected by what had happened and, unfastening his own cloak, he cast it upon the body and covered it. And then he sent the dead King back to Persepolis in royal state for burial. It may be that the grave in which the butchered body was placed should be recognized in the unfinished rock-cut sepulchre which can be found in a low-lying cliff to the south of the palace.

It was now July, 330 BC, and Alexander had usurped the empire of the Persian Achaemenids save for its extension to the Jaxartes in the north and through the Hindu Kush into the hills and plains of the Punjab in the south-east. This far-reaching promontory of empire in India is of high importance to our present theme, and briefly we must in due course follow Alexander's devious and adventurous path to its extremity. But first something more must be said of the great palace of Persepolis, and of the background of the momentous burning which has occupied this first chapter and is in effect the centre of our story.

NAQSH-I-RUSTAM
near Persepolis: rock-cut tomb of Darius II (424–405 BC)

29

THE
PALACE

The palace of Persepolis stood, and intelligible vestiges still stand, upon a broad terrace of limestone levelled and compensated by artifice at the foot of the Kuh-i-Rahmat, the Mountain of Mercy, which overlooks the Persepolis plain from the east (page 11). There is evidence that this kind of siting had been used in the Persian homeland of Khuzistan. Certainly a commanding terrace, though without the impending mountain, was the basis of the palace which Cyrus the Great began in the middle of the sixth century BC at Pasargadae, fifty miles north of Persepolis (page 51). He held Pasargadae in honour, says Strabo, 'because he there conquered Astyages the Mede in his last battle, and so transferred to himself the empire of Asia'.

Recent exploration (1963–5) at Pasargadae has revealed the general aspect of this predecessor of Persepolis. A great masonry platform, approached by two staircases, crowns a hill above a plain upon which are the widely scattered fragments of a gatehouse, a garden pavilion, a small residential palace, and a tower-like structure known as 'Solomon's Prison', which may have been some sort of temple or sacred strong-room. Of a permanent town there is no sign, and it is supposed that the population, still very near to its ancestral nomadism, lived in tents. The shallow valley adjoining the palace-platform is enclosed by a substantial mud-brick wall with square towers; it was presumably intended to contain the royal retainers and craftsmen. A mile and a half to the south in lonely grandeur stands the tomb of the great Cyrus himself, once filled with treasure and

PERSEPOLIS:
*air-view of the great
palace of Darius I and
Xerxes, about 510–460*
BC (*North to the top*)

34

surrounded by a grove of trees with lush grass and running water. Empty, it remains in its desert a simple and worthy monument to one of the outstanding men of history (page 33).

The building of the principal palace on the platform of Pasargadae was never begun by Cyrus and continued to lapse in the time of his son Cambyses, who was distracted by the task of conquering Egypt. The third Great King, Darius I, decided to move to Persepolis, but built upon the Pasargadae platform an extensive mud-brick structure within a fortification of similar material (page 51, top). The structure, which included a courtyard, may have served as a temporary residence for the King or his governor, and have become thereafter a military depot and provincial headquarters. It was burned, probably by Alexander's troops, then partially rebuilt in trivial fashion, and finally destroyed about 280 BC, perhaps in an uprising on the death of Alexander's eastern successor, Seleucus I. The details are of no matter here; the present importance of the place is that it was a tentative, immature forerunner of the Persepolitan palace, in which Achaemenid art was to reach its apogee.

At Persepolis, work was inaugurated by Darius in the years following 520 BC and was continued successively by Xerxes and Artaxerxes I until about 460 BC. The duplication of some of its elements may be a result of this protracted operation but does not mar an essentially coherent plan. Towards the north were two formal gateways, admitting to two richly columned halls; towards the south were residential buildings and a large treasury. The whole assemblage was set within towered defences of mud brick and approached by monumental staircases, richly pictured in relief.

The place was on a scale worthy of a mighty empire at its prime, a work of high originality, designed and carved with assured mastery. The bare bones of the two vast halls today do little more than hint at former splendour. The western, begun by Darius before 513, was two hundred feet square internally, and its thirty-six columns carried the timber roof at a height of some sixty feet above the floor. At every corner stood a substantial mud-brick tower for guards and attendants; and there is evidence that a part of the exterior of these towers bore inscriptions in tiles, glazed, and of white and turquoise colours. Doors, and possibly other parts of the structure, were rivetted with ornamental bronze plates: rosettes and the representation of a griffin are mentioned, and gold-covered nails. Of the columns something will be said later. It has been calculated, a trifle ambitiously, that ten thousand people could be packed into the hall. Certainly a very considerable crowd of courtiers, guards, petitioners and envoys could be assembled here, but curiously there is no indication of the whereabouts of the throne, and the square plan of the hall would seem to have dispersed rather than focused ceremony.

To the east of this Hall of Audience, Xerxes and his successor raised a yet larger hall, 230 feet square internally, with towers or guard-rooms flanking the entrance-portico towards the north. The roof was supported upon no less than a hundred columns, a round number which was to recur at more than one period in later Indian architecture. The excavators named the building the 'Throne Hall', largely because of the scenes sculptured on the northern and southern door-jambs, where the Great King is shown ceremonially seated (page 21). Subsequently, the same modern authorities preferred the view that the hall was intended to display the greatest of the royal treasures, 'and thus to relieve congestion in the old Treasury [which lay behind the hall], and make room for further tribute and booty expected to flow to the heart of the Empire'. In other words, it was a sort of Royal Museum and overflow-storehouse. This I find hard to believe. Thinking back from much later Persian custom, it may be recalled that in the sixteenth century the king had at his disposal *two* halls of audience: a private and a public one, respectively for the more personal reception of friends, nobles and special envoys, and for public business including the sentencing and even the execution of criminals. I see no reason why this Moghul custom should not have been rooted in Achaemenid tradition.

Where the general scheme of these great halls came from, no one knows. There is no clear precedent. Such halls as survive at Pasargadae are of a relatively meagre kind and, incidentally, are oblong, not square. The invention of the vast square hall must, it seems, like so much else, be ascribed to the genius of the architects and sculptors of Darius I, before and after 500 BC.

And indeed nothing could have been more expressive of the ethos of the great Empire. Let it be said again that in those gigantic halls there was no determined architectural vista, nothing to lead the eye or mind onward. They were in fact petrified groves, as though in each of them a Persian paradise had been turned to stone. The whole sense of the buildings was static, as is that of the long, repetitive processions of carved soldiers and tribute-bearers which flank the staircases (pages 38–9). If they move at all, these regimented figures, it is as in a dream. The great simulacra of the King which here and there occur in stiff and formal pose are frozen, or turned to gold as by the touch of a Midas. There is no place here for emotion or individuality, still less for anything approaching inspiration and abandon. In all this there is no tomorrow; here was verily a land in which it was always afternoon. In short, it was the elaborated consummation and end of a brief and forced tradition. In vivid contrast, the milling quarrelsome crowd of Europeans who now for a moment surged through this fossil land in the train of Alexander was full of a noisy unfulfilment and aspiration; theirs was the future. To this conflict between East and West we shall return. But first a few more factual details of the scene.

36

PERSEPOLIS:
*eastern stairway to the
Hall of Audience, lined
by Persian guards*

PERSEPOLIS:
*reconstructed capital
surmounted by
addorsed bulls*

PERSEPOLIS:
*Lotus-capital on jamb
of a doorway into the
'Throne Hall'*

The main bulk of the palace-buildings at Persepolis was of mud brick, which has long since dissolved. Occasional tile-veneering has been mentioned. Major doorways and window-frames were of limestone, the surface of which was often highly polished; a feature which again we shall observe significantly in Mauryan India, heir of Achaemenid Persia. And there is yet another aspect of Persian construction which seems to have travelled eastwards. The Persepolitan masons were quite casual in their use of stone blocks. Their stone window-frames, for example, 'are not built up logically, as was done in Egypt or Greece, from four separate pieces: lintel, sill, and two jambs. They are sometimes carved in a single block; at other times parts, one-half or three-quarters of the circumferences, were cut from one block and the rest from one or more separate pieces. In other words, the stone was treated in the manner of a sculptor, not that of a mason. The same odd treatment is observed in the stairs; these are not regular units cut in quantities and used in a set fashion, a number of identical blocks for the treads and a number of blocks to build the parapet, but it is the rule that an arbitrary width and length of steps is hewn out of the same block with part of the parapet. In a similar way columns are never made of a fixed number of drums of a given size.' These unusual structural details (quoted from Herzfeld and Frankfort) are here recounted for reasons which will appear in a later chapter (page 135).

For the moment it will suffice that those columns are bizarre inventions, not closely like any in the West but parental to others which we will find

PERSEPOLIS:
*column-capital of
addorsed bulls from the
Hall of Audience*

in the further East. Some of them were of wood, plastered and gaily painted with oblique spiral patterns. Others, of stone, had bell-shaped bases with floral detail and capitals faintly akin to the palm-leaf, papyrus and lotus capitals of Egypt but surmounted by individual imposts of addorsed fore-parts of lions, bulls or bull-men (see above). We shall see the descendants of these intricate and imaginative concepts in India; and some of their elements will recur in the next chapter in partial comparison with exceptional capitals in the West.

Of the Mediterranean West however, there is very little indeed in the Achaemenid architecture of Persepolis, if we except a hint of Egypt. At the time when Darius and Xerxes were building tinder for the torches of Alexander, there were no palaces worthy of the name in the Greek world. There, men of all kinds lived in small stone or mud houses. Burglars were 'wall-diggers'. No Greek boasted of the house of Pericles. Palaces were to find their way westwards into the Hellenistic world after Alexander, but centuries later even the Emperor Augustus, ruler of the Roman world, lived on the Palatine in relatively simple dignity. Royal ostentation was an Eastern notion.

Of the sculptures of Persepolis, the carved processions of soldiers and tribute-bearers which march beside the staircases, I have said little here, although they are the surviving triumph of the palace. They belong essentially to the background of the burning, and will appear more aptly in the next chapter.

41

THE
BACKGROUND
OF THE
BURNING

previous page
PERSEPOLIS:
*figures from the
eastern stairway of the
Hall of Audience
representing foreigners,
probably from
Gandhara, bringing
tribute to the King*

44

PERSEPOLIS:
*approach to the Hall of Audience, showing
to the left a Median nobleman and to the
right a Persian carrying a flower (lotus?)*

For the background of the great burning we look westwards, and in more senses than one. The destroyer of Persepolis was a Macedonian but would have called himself a Greek; did he not claim descent from Heracles, if not from Zeus himself? The carved masterpiece which he destroyed derived also from the West, though in a more neighbourly sense, from Assyria and the Twin Rivers; it is the last and most easterly, and today the most eloquent, monument of its kind. The builders of Persepolis had thought to bring the orient into Europe; instead, the destroyers of Persepolis brought Europe into the orient and, incidentally and paradoxically, in a fashion to be explored in later chapters, scattered the disjecta of the Persian mode across the further East. Whilst all this was happening a new politic and sociology, a wide new outlook on life, were in the making. And the instrument of this Eurasian revolution was a youngster in his twenties, from the West.

In an earlier chapter it has been recalled how in 480 BC the flames of Persepolis had been anticipated by the conflagration of another capital: of Athens itself, then the most civilized city of Europe. Briefly, in that year – another of the cardinal years of history – the vast armies of Xerxes had overrun the little state of Attica and in so doing had threatened the whole future of the continent. The story has of course been a classic for two dozen centuries. In response, as it seemed, to a dubious direction from the Delphic oracle, that far-seeing Zeus would provide them with a wooden wall as a defence, most of the Athenians took refuge in their ships and, with others,

45

ultimately broke the Persian fleet at Salamis. But a few of them, simple-minded temple-caretakers and labourers, stayed upon the Acropolis and fenced it roughly with logs – a more literal interpretation of the oracle. The Persians, as Herodotus tells us, occupied the neighbouring Hill of Ares, the Areopagus, and thence attacked the barricade with flaming arrows. Eventually they penetrated the improvised defence, and 'when they had laid low the defenders they plundered the temple and burnt the whole Acropolis'.

The temple referred to may have been the Erechtheum in its previous embodiment, but was more probably that which was to be known in after-years as the Parthenon. At the time, this towering shrine and treasury of Athens was being rebuilt in marble and was standing half-finished amidst its inflammable scaffolding. Its platform, incorporated a generation later in the new Parthenon by the architects of Pericles, still bears at its western end the scars of the flames of Xerxes; and its discarded column-drums can be seen in the marginal wall of the Acropolis where they were embedded as building-material after the Persian withdrawal. Like Persepolis, the Acropolis shows its wounds.

And those wounds were not confined to the Acropolis or to Athens. Throughout Attica the Persians left a trail of destruction behind them. What in Athens escaped the wrath of Xerxes himself was finally deleted in the following year by his general Mardonius, who lit the fires afresh. Temples in particular were the objects of Persian mischief. And thereafter for thirty years after the invasion their blackened ruins remained throughout the land as monuments of hate; for on the eve of the decisive battle of Plataea at which in 479 the Persians were driven out of Europe, the quarrelsome Greek patriots, for the moment more or less united, swore solemnly not to rebuild those sorry memorials. The sequel is again familiar but, like a well-worn children's tale, it bears infinite repetition.

At first sight, indeed, the whole episode in the pages of the Greek historians is liable to emerge to the modern eye as an odd mixture of ill-conducted nursery and heroic achievement, acted theatrically upon a minute patch of the earth's surface. But let the more modern historian beware of hasty belittlement. In this twentieth century our diminishing world is itself in relative size scarcely larger than classical Hellas. International intrigue and conflict, fickle loyalties and almost universal opportunism, barely relieved by tiny flashes of principle or sentiment, remain today astonishingly close to the political and moral condition of the Greek world in the fifth century BC. After all, Washington is in time-space nearer to Moscow than Athens was to Sparta, and their mutual sentiments are much the same. On the mechanics of the business, Peking could today invade Europe in a fraction of the time taken by the hosts of Xerxes for a similar operation across the Hellespont. And who knows what European mercenaries we should find in the ranks of a hostile China, successors to the 50,000 Greeks who stood, as Herodotus tells us, in the Persian ranks at Plataea? As for those incessant, malicious and fatiguing bickerings among the Hellenic states, have we not after all our own United Nations! And what right or cause has the historian to patronize those fifth-century Greeks who could forget Themistocles (as another nation chose to forget Churchill) after a critical war in which he was their principal saviour? Or could afford that profligacy of the spirit which permitted them to consign their immortal sculptor to a death in gaol, and perpetuate their philosopher with a draught of hemlock? No, the historic drama of the Greeks was already enacted on a full-size stage, and our own is relatively no larger, certainly no grander.

But to return. For that thirty years after Plataea, the Athenians adhered to their Plataean vow. The wreckage on the Acropolis, and elsewhere in Attica, remained in studied ruin, like the British Residency at Lucknow. That it should do so no doubt jumped with the immediate post-war economy, in which the restoration of Attic agriculture and shipping and much military construction demanded exacting priority. But by the middle of the century a new generation had arisen; by the year 450 men of thirty, in the full flush of early middle age, had no first-hand experience of the Persian wars; on the contrary, it may be supposed that they were sick and tired of the repetitive war-stories of their fathers and grandfathers. We in our time know all about the tedium of those hang-overs which have lost their immediate context and have not yet assumed the dignity of history. The Plataean oath was already meaningless or even forgotten. The Mood was ripe. The time had come to clear up the mess.

Then, in this newly creative Mood, there happened one of those rare miracles: a miraculous instant when everything combined to produce a masterpiece. The Mood coincided precisely with the Man, the Means, and the Moment.

The Man was of course Pericles, of whom Thucydides and Plutarch have left a convincing picture. By personal prowess he became in effect 'the aristocrat of Athens', liable on occasion to popular questioning but beyond all question the intellectual visionary of the Athenian renaissance: heir in some measure to the 'tyrants' of the sixth century but, within a basically democratic setting, at the same time already in part foreshadowing the more enlightened of the autocrats of the era of Alexander's successors. He was a genius, and a master of geniuses (page 48).

Genius is prone to take a risk with morals. In 454 Pericles transferred from Delos to the Acropolis of Athens the treasury which the Delian League had assembled on the sacred and central island as an insurance against a repetition of the Persian peril. Here, whether properly or not, were the Means for the exercise of genius; in terms of the time, almost

unlimited wealth for the glorification of the city which had, with Sparta, led the resistance to the invader and was now indulging a reaction of extravagant self-esteem. We need not take the case to the Court of Appeal and plead righteously that all this substance should legally have been squandered upon futile preparations for a war that no longer threatened. The fact remains: the Means were found.

And then, the Moment. Within the first fifty years of the fifth century Greek art passed with increasing impetus through the last phases of archaism, and by 450 was poised upon the threshold of fulfilment. At Olympia in the western Peloponnese, the Plataean oath did not run.

There no sacrosanct ruins stood as a bar to architectural and sculptural progress. The take-over of Olympia by the state of Elis in 471 BC from that of Pisa, which had previously controlled the site and its accruing revenues, offered a context for the fashioning of a great new temple of Zeus. The building arose in the years before and after 460 – midway between the Persian sack of the Athenian Acropolis and the reconstruction of the Parthenon. Its famous sculptures survive sufficiently to show us the condition of Greek monumental art precisely at the time when architectural sculpture in Attica was at a standstill. And they are exactly true to their median position: still a trifle stiff or orthostatic, still a little uncertain in the modelling and interrelationship of muscle and drapery, still lacking in full freedom and confidence. Meanwhile at Athens, competent and experimental sculptors were rapidly bringing their art to full maturity: Myron, Pythagoras, Polycleitus and others. The Moment had at last arrived for the epiphany of the great master who could finally gather together all these converging threads and weave them into the perfect pattern. The Moment had arrived for Pheidias. Had he and Pericles lived twenty years earlier or twenty years later, they would have missed it.

The Mood, the Man, the Means, the Moment; it was a perfect synchronism. No more need be said of this here, save to recall the consummate judgment with which Plutarch appraises the astonishing achievement of Pericles and his colleagues, not least in the incredible speed with which their task was executed: 'Whence the greater is the marvel of the works of Pericles, that they were wrought in an instant for long time. For each one of them in its beauty was instantly (as it were) of seasoned age, while even to the present day remaining new and in the full flush of youth. Thus it blooms in perpetual freshness, appearing to the eye untouched by time as though the whole work had been infused with an undiminishing breath of life and an ageless spirit.' To this it is only fair to add that any English rendering limps clumsily after Plutarch's terse and nervous Greek.

Of course, as often in history, there is in all this an under-plot of paradox. The culminating inspiration of Greek artistry found its full and final expression in (and let us not underrate this) the most expensive temple in the Greek world only when a foreign invader had ruthlessly swept away the past and had left behind him an equally ruthless challenge for the future; a challenge which eventually found a simultaneous response in concentrated talent and concentrated wealth. In due course we shall see that a century and a half later the destroyers of Persepolis rendered a not incomparable service in the East. Like Xerxes, the Attic courtesan and her king wrought better than they knew. In the act of simulating Xerxes they were in fact founding, like him, a new age of achievement. Before we turn eastward to this, however, the western background commands another glance.

At the moment when Xerxes, seated upon his throne under a hill opposite Salamis, saw his navy shattered by the Greeks, his builders were still at work far away upon the great palace which his father had begun at Persepolis. It may be accepted that there, as at Susa, where Darius in his famous building-inscription of 494–490 BC proclaims that 'the stone-cutters who wrought the stone, those were Ionians and Sardians', his craftsmen included Greeks from western Asia, precursors of the sorry throng which Alexander encountered on his entry into Persia. It may even be that his chief sculptor engaged upon these works was the Greek Telephanes, of whom Pliny (*Nat. Hist.* XXXIV, 68) tells us that, although ranked by ancient critics with Polycleitus, Myron and Pythagoras, he remained practically unknown (in the West) 'because he devoted himself to the workshops of kings Xerxes and Darius'. This sort of supra-national interchange was common enough in the Asian world down to and including Islamic times. It cut freely across wars, politics, ideologies and other loyalties, and must be reconsidered in the present setting.

First, however, a word as to the generalities of Persian (Achaemenid) art. The Persians themselves were traditionally nomads, equipped adequately, no doubt, with that limited range of mobile craftsmanship which is apt to nomadism, but with no sort of skill in the monumental and static arts. It was a major moment of crisis therefore when between 559 and 529 BC, under the inspired leadership of the great Cyrus, they took over the vast composite civilization of the Middle East from the Mediterranean to Media, and suddenly found themselves with the weight of the world upon their shoulders: Lydians, Carians, Lycians, Babylonians, peripheral Greeks and, above all, the substantial shadow of that immense Assyrian Empire which, with the Tigris as its axis, the newly subject Medes, leagued with Babylonia, had acquired at the end of the previous century. It was a gigantic burden for a people accustomed to travelling light; a burden comparable in anticipation with that which the Kushana nomads in Afghanistan and India were to assume under not dissimilar conditions in the first and second century AD, or that which the Muslim swarms were to encounter in Asia, Africa and Europe during the seventh and eighth centuries AD. The burden was not lightened when Cambyses, son and successor of Cyrus, added Egypt to the bundle.

In the forefront of the Persian problem was the inheritance (at one remove) of the mature and closely co-ordinated culture of Assyria. The result was a foregone conclusion: in its main ideas the new Persian Empire took shape as the effective successor of the old Assyrian Empire. Its monumental art was first and foremost Assyrian in inspiration, modified by two factors. First, the Persians were not Assyrians and inevitably transmuted, however subconsciously and incompletely, the alien traditions which they had adopted. Secondly, the Persians were not themselves trained craftsmen

opposite

PERSEPOLIS:
south stairway of palace begun by Darius, showing servants bringing provisions for the king's table

NINEVEH:
North Palace: Ashurbanipal, uncrowned, hunting lions, c. 650 BC. A good example of the 'linear' sculpture of Assyria, contrasting with the more emphatic modelling of Persia.
(British Museum)

in the new sense, and were necessarily at the mercy, in however limited a measure, of the miscellaneous technicians – Ionians, Sardians, Egyptians, Medes – whom they are recorded to have employed.

In this situation attempts have been made by modern scholarship to discover and proclaim the influence of Ionian or Greek employees upon the Assyrio-Persian art of Susa and Persepolis. Assyrian sculpture was essentially sculpture in relief, but relief of a linear kind with little emphasis upon modelling. Henri Frankfort aptly dubbed it 'reinforced drawing'; drapery, for instance, was largely indicated by unrealistic two-dimensional conventions, though with close attention to ornamental detail. On the other hand the scenes depicted, whether of hunting or warfare or of a more domestic character, are lively and varied. They tell a story and are full of observed moments (see above).

PERSEPOLIS:
reliefs on eastern stairway to the Hall of Audience. Upper register: *delegation of Cilicians (?) led by Persian usher and bringing two rams.* Lower register: *Cappadocians (?) led by Median usher and bringing a bridled stallion, overcoat, coat and trousers*

The reliefs of Persepolis incline to the opposite of both these conventions. The monotonously repetitive figures and scenes of the great stairways tell no story save that of tributary wealth and the regimented grandeur of the imperial court. The endless and rather tiresome processions have the quality of sub-architectural ornaments. They have indeed been compared with the recurrent patterning of oriental rugs. There is nothing 'Greek' about all this; here we have the imposed conventions of a rigid, impersonal hierarchy. However derivative from Assyria in general presentation and in much of its detail, it is in spirit Persian (page 55).

As against this, other features have been ascribed to influences from the Greek West. Notable among these is a tendency at Persepolis to lend a robust, three-dimensional quality to the reliefs. Animals, human beings, drapery are rendered boldly, if with a tedious repetition. The rendering is plastic in a sense that is not applicable to Assyrian art as a whole. Within the Assyrian framework, this has been hailed as a Greek importation.

Well, it may be. But when Miss Gisela Richter quotes with approval Coomaraswamy's judgment that 'Achaemenid art . . . survives as documentary illustration of a moment of real and intimate relationship between Asia and Europe', I part company. To me, whatever importance a Greek element or two may have assumed in the Persepolitan workshops – whatever sketch of a Hellenizing bearded head some expatriate Greek workman may have scratched obscurely upon the stone slipper of a Darius in the palace there (page 19) – very little that was truly Greek went to the making of those great friezes of impassively marshalled figures or those tall, palmlike columns that can still be seen upon the palace-platform. When another scholar observes that 'there must have been a good few Greek artisans engaged on this work; and the master who adapted their inbred idioms to the cosmopolitan pageantry of Persian imperialism must have been an artist of considerable creative vision, comparable to the designer of the Parthenon frieze at Athens' – when I read that, I find myself sorrowfully

rejecting the implication. The Parthenon and Persepolis are poles apart in every sort of fashion; in spiritual descent they are each the impact of an utterly different ethos. Their only valid common factor is that within half a century both in their divers ways immortalized state processions.

No; it is the essential differences between the Greek and the Persian modes that matter. To recapitulate: the sculptors of the Parthenon were running free; the Panathenaic frieze is a romp (page 56). It is full of triumphs, full too of the mistakes which greatness can afford and throws away as stimuli to lesser talent. The sculptors of Persepolis (with all allowance for a more archaic age) were in comparison clamped down under gaol-guard; their creations are patterns rather than persons – repetitive and tediously impassive. Through and through, the Greeks were significantly Europeans, the Persians Asiatics. True, within the sixth century the Greeks of the Anatolian seaboard were long enough under the autocratic rule of Lydians and Persians to incur certain debts to Asia. The political discipline imposed upon them by the Asian way of life, though mitigated by the freedom of the seas, no doubt contributed to the development of organized urban life and of methodical scientific introspection on a scale which was not matched on the Greek mainland until the following century. Artistically, on the other hand, Asian contacts after the seventh century offered singularly little to the Greek fine arts and architecture. The Greeks were tumultuously alive and were blundering their way to perfection. The Persians were prim and content and used up. It may be that in architecture the multiple straight-stemmed column-capitals of Persepolis were at long range organically related to one of the seventh century at Old Smyrna and with those of the sixth-century Massalian treasury at Delphi, or were in parental relationship with others of much later date in the Athenian stoa of Attalus and elsewhere. If so, whether the inspiration was primarily Ionic or Persian is a problem for academic discussion. Leaving aside this detail, however, let it be repeated that in art-forms of the classical period the dying East and the adult West owed to each other little of significant value.

On that night, then, in the spring of 330 B C when flames reddened the sky over Persepolis, the Macedonian had lighted a funeral-pyre that was ready for his torch. In Persepolis there perished in that moment an era of Middle-Eastern civilization that had outlived – if it had ever fully discovered – creative impulse. The great age of the Assyrian and Persian empires was at an end – and it is no chance that those mournful, immobile processions of laboriously chiselled and polished soldiers and sycophants beside the stairways of the palace have about them a semblance of the pageantry of death (page 54).

And yet, as the sequel was to show, this was not quite finality. In due course, other vagabonds from the inexhaustible reserves of central Asia would replace the Persians and establish new and fruitful contacts with the

classical West. Meanwhile, by a curious twist of fortune, in the eastward track of Alexander the ultimate heirs of Achaemenid culture were to find a distant refuge beyond the mountains. There, as we shall see, a strangely alien patronage awaited them.

PERSEPOLIS:
the Gate of Xerxes with its guardian bulls

ΣΕΒΕΙΝ ΔΙΣΤΕΡΡΣΤΕΙΑΚΑΤ...ΛΛΑΣΑΣ ΤΑΣΔΙΑΤΡΙΒΑΣΕ
ΟΞΑΝΓΛΛΣΗΣ ΕΓΚΡΑΤΗΣΗΙΚΑΙΜΗΤΕΕΛ ΤΟΥΣ...
ΤΕ ΜΗΔΕΝΟΣΚΕΝΟΙΓΑΡΕΣΤΙΝΚΑΙ ΕΝ...Λ ΑΙΣΑ
ΜΗ ΕΓΕΝΚΑΤΑΠΑΝΤΑΤΡΟΠΟΝΤΑΥΤΑΔΕ ΗΩΝΤΕ
ΤΕΛΑ ΑΝΑΚ ΝΤ Α ΠΑΡΑΒΑΙΝΟΝΤΕΣΔΕ ΑΥ ΑΔΙΚΑΕ
ΠΕ ΣΑΠΕΧΘΟΝ ΤΑΙΟ ΔΑΝΕΑΤΤΟΥΣΕΠΑΙΝΛΣΙΝΤΟΥΣΔΕΠ
ΔΙΑΠΓΑΤΟΝΤΑΙΟΥΛΟΜΕΝΟΙ ΠΑΡΑΤΟΥΣΛΙ ΟΥΣΕ ΛΑΜ
ΕΑΥΤΟΥΣ ΤΟΕ Ε ΔΕΑΛΛΗΛΟΥΣΘΑΥΜΑΞΕΙΝΚΑΙΤΑΑΛΛΗΥ
ΤΑΥΤΑΔΕ Ο ΟΥΝΤΕΣΤΟΛΥΜΑΡΟΣ ΤΕΡΟΙ ΕΣΟ ΤΑ Α ΑΑ
ΕΚΑΣΤ ΣΑΥΤΛΝΕΠΙΣΤΑΤ ΚΑΙ ΤΟΙΣΠΑΥΤΑ ΕΓΕΚΟΥΣ
ΑΜΕΙΝ ΣΙΝΔΙΑΠΑΝΤΟΣΕΥΣΕΒΟΥΝΤΕΣ Ο ΑΟ ΜΕΤΕΙΒ
ΚΑ ΕΣΤΡΕΠΤΑΙΤΗΝΚΑΛΗ ΗΝΗΝΕ ΔΗΜΕΝΑΚΑΙΕΞΗΤ
ΜΥΡΙΑΔΕΣΔΕΚΑ ΕΝΤΕΚΑΙΑΝΑΘΕΟΗΣΑΝ ΑΛΛΑΙΜΥΡΙΑΔΕ
ΤΟΙΕΤΕΛΕΥΤΗΣΑΝΑΠΕΞΕΙΝΟΥ ΤΟΥΧΡΟΝΟΥΟΛΕΟΣΚΑΙΟΙΚΤΟ
ΦΙΣΥ Σ ΠΟΥΣΕΚΕΛΕΥΕΝΑΠΕΧΕΣΘΛΙΤΑΝΕΥΤΥΧΛΝΣΓΟΥ
ΠΟΙΕΥΣΕΒΕΑΣ ΚΑΙ ΟΥΤΟΕΤΙΔΥΣ ΘΡΕΣ ΕΡΣΝΥΠΕΙΛΩ
Λ ΜΕΓΑΙΝΕΡΑ ΟΓΑΙΝΚΑΙΑΛΛΟΙΤΙΝΕΣΟΙΠΕΡΙΠΑΝΕΤΣΕΞΕΙΑ
ΗΤΑΣΕΔ Α Α ΠΑΣΑΕΛΣΣΥΜΦΟΡΟΝ ΤΑΡ ΘΕΙΝΚΑΙΛΙΔΑΣ
ΕΓΑΙΣΧΥ Α ΑΙΘΛΥΜΑΞΕΙΝ ΦΙΛΟΥΣΚΑΙΕΤΑΙΡΟΥΣΑ
ΑΟΥΛΟ ΣΡΑΙΜΙΣ ΠΤΟΙΣΛΕΚΟΥΛΟ Α Α ΟΛΣ Ο ΤΟΥΤΩΝ
Λ ΤΙΣ ΤΕΝΗΚΕΝΗΣΞΗΚΤΑΙΚΑΙΤΟΥΤΟ ΠΑΡΑ ΑΟΡ
Ι ΝΕΥΣΣΑ ΣΔΑΕ ΤΟΥΤΟΙΣΕΑ ΣΝ Τ ΝΕΝΚΑΙΟΤ ΕΝ

AFTER THE BURNING: 1

NEW DISCOVERIES IN BACTRIA AND ITS ENVIRONS

So much for the Western background to the conflagration of Persepolis. In effect, the event marked the end of what may be called the Graeco-Persian episode: an episode distinguished by a symmetry such as Clio does not always exhibit. It had begun with the destructive invasion of Europe at the will of the first Darius who was also the first builder of the Persepolitan palace. It now ended with the counter-invasion of Persia by Europe in the last days of the last Darius, and culminated in the great burning. The story might seem to be rounded and complete.

And so in a sense it was. Persepolis in 330 BC saw the end of an era. But by the same token it also saw the beginning of another. In that year, Alexander paused at the middle point of his great adventure – middle point in time and space. He had crossed the Hellespont in 334, and was to turn back from the Punjab in 326. At Persepolis he had behind him two thousand miles of urbanized Asia; in front of him lay two thousand miles of desert, steppe and mountain, with an ultimate fringe of settled living, but mostly a quicksand of nomadic or semi-nomadic villagers and tent-dwellers. Here, to the East, new problems awaited his statesmanship no less than his generalship. In many ways it was here that Alexander's genius showed its most enduring qualities. And Persepolis was the turning-point. The cliché is justified; Persepolis is one of the landmarks of history.

To trace the sequel of Persepolis is to explore two of Alexander's greatest achievements: the systematic civilization of the wild eastern regions of the old Persian Empire; and the resultant creation of a civilized continuum through a multitude of nations and cultures from the Mediterranean to the Ganges. That continuum has never since been completely broken. No other single creative act in world-history – unless the European discovery of America – has in so short a time matched this astonishing triumph.

First, in the tracks of Alexander we move rapidly if circuitously from the ruins of the great palace and the paltry obsequies of the last Persian king towards the north-eastern limit of the Persian Empire beside the Jaxartes, partly across uncharted country full of Parthians and a miscellany of Scythians or Sakas and other folk, and partly along the royal roads laid out by Cyrus and his successors. On the way Alexander looped sharply southwards through Herat and Seistan, and thence north-eastwards through Kandahar (of which, more anon), Kabul and the Hindu Kush to Bactria in what is now northern Afghanistan. There the satrap Bessus, who had been at least partly responsible for the murder of Darius, had assumed the trappings of the Persian king and was collecting an army of resistance. On the approach of Alexander, he fled across the Oxus but was shortly delivered up to his enemy and was eventually, after oriental torture, executed at Ecbatana. His principal crime had been that of usurping the usurper's crown.

Meanwhile Alexander had sped northwards to the Jaxartes and his inherited frontier. On the way he reduced the high-walled Persian frontier-city of Cyropolis and seven fortresses also established by Cyrus the Great between that and the river; and, in the face of trouble from the nomad Scythians of the borderland, he founded on the river-bank, as counterpart to Cyropolis, his 'Furthest Alexandria' (*Alexandria Eschate*), the modern Chodjend, to serve, in the words of Arrian, as 'an excellent base for a possible future invasion of Scythia and as a defence against raiding tribes from across the river'. Alexander himself 'spent twenty days on the work of fortifying his new town, and arranged for the settlement there of any Greek mercenaries and neighbouring tribesmen who wished to avail themselves of the opportunity, and also of a number of Macedonians no longer fit for active service. To mark the occasion, after his customary religious ceremonies he held games with athletic and equestrian contests.' The picture is no doubt representative of many other episodes of the kind.

And here it is appropriate to recall that the basis of Alexander's colonial policy, like that of the Romans after him, was the building or reshaping of towns after the traditional Greek pattern. He conquered by civilizing, by sowing 'Alexandrias' as he went, particularly in the uneasy wastelands of Asia. His Furthest Alexandria on the Jaxartes has just been mentioned, but that was 'Furthest' or 'Last' only in the sense that it confirmed the old

Persian line along the river as his own ultimate border in those parts. Geographically his remotest Alexandria was founded in 326, when, in the last stage of his adventure, he left the Hindu Kush behind him and struck deep into the Punjab. There, on the left bank of the Jhelum river, he established Alexandria Bucephala to commemorate the death of his famous war-horse Bucephalus, before facing the vicissitudes of his long return to Babylon. The exact site of the city on the Jhelum has not been identified.

Plutarch tells us that in all more than seventy cities were founded by the conqueror. The number need not be exact, but it is certain that, of one kind or another, his foundations were numerous. They might be full-blown cities of the Greek type; Alexandria-by-Egypt and Alexandria Eschate were of this sort. They might be adaptations of, or supplements to, existing native towns; such probably was the new Bactra, established as an Alexandria beside the old provincial capital. They might be more or less evanescent garrison-posts, planted perhaps (but not necessarily) in the vicinity of a native village. The eminent William Tarn, in an elaborate and unnecessary argument, sought to regard Kandahar, which has commonly been regarded as reflecting the actual name 'Alexandria', as such a post; arbitrarily degrading it to 'Alexandropolis' with the wholly unwarranted comment that a place so-called 'cannot have been a city founded by Alexander' and was 'at best a military colony'. But here, without more ado, I pause to draw attention to new evidence not available when Tarn was writing.

Somewhere hereabouts, if not at Kandahar then within a reasonable distance of it, Alexander established an Alexandria in Arachosia, a broad region of Baluchistan behind the Quetta hills. For conjectural reasons which need not here be repeated, Tarn preferred to find this foundation 'without any doubt' at Ghazni, some two hundred miles north-east of Kandahar. No physical evidence for any such Alexandria-Ghazni has ever been recognized, though in the absence of systematic search this default cannot be stressed. On the other hand, at the rejected Kandahar in 1958 and 1963 two very important inscriptions were brought to light and alter the situation. Both bear the title of the great Buddhist emperor Ashoka, the Mauryan emperor who governed most of India approximately from 268 to 233 BC. In the north-west his empire included Arachosia as one of the border-satrapies ceded to his grandfather Chandragupta, the first Mauryan king, by Alexander's successor Seleucus.

To establish these inscriptions in context it may be recalled that Ashoka, at heart a saintly fanatic, having begun his reign by slaughtering a hundred thousand wretches in Orissa, turned with equal thoroughness to humanitarianism, and as a Buddhist convert inflicted charity relentlessly upon his subjects and his neighbours. The first of the two new inscriptions, carved on rock, is duplicated in Greek and Aramaic (page 67). The latter was an official language of Achaemenid Persia and was therefore traditionally appropriate to the region; but here the Greek takes precedence above the Aramaic and occupies two-thirds of the inscribed space. It runs to fourteen lines and is complete (page 69); the Aramaic text, in smaller lettering, is also complete and runs to eight lines.

Though not specifically dated, the double inscription is shown by its content to reflect a part of the fourteen Major Rock Edicts whereby the converted Buddhist emperor broadcast his precepts, particularly in the northern and north-western parts of his immense empire, in the years adjoining 255 BC. With this date, analysis of the severe and monumental Greek lettering by Louis Robert is wholly consistent; it points to the third century BC with a bias towards the middle of the century. Language and style are authentically and scholastically Hellenistic, and the persistent tendency to link phrases with the word *kai* ('and') is a recognized formalism of priestly Greek. Here is Hellas authoritatively *in partibus*.

But not so the import of the proclamation – for such it is. Here is the thinking, not of the Western world, but of the Orient and, particularly, of India. It reads thus:

Ten years having been fulfilled, the king Piodasses ['The Beneficent', honorific by-name of Ashoka] has demonstrated Piety to mankind. And from this he has made mankind more pious, and all things prosper throughout the world. And the king abstains from living things, and all other men and the hunters and indeed the fishers of the king have ceased to kill. And any who lacked control have ceased from their weakness to the best of their power. And they have become obedient to father and mother and to their elders, contrary to previous custom. And in future, acting thus, they will live better and more laudably in all things.

This quiet and searching selflessness, with its underlying quality of negation, is native to the homeland of the Buddha. Its mood is incompletely in tune with that of the terse and virile Greek in which the expatriate epigrapher has expressed it. In his Western idiom he has interpreted rather than mirrored the original Sanskrit or Prakrit that no doubt lay before him. Even though his matter savour of the Orient, his utterance is truly Greek. It has been pointed out by Louis Robert that the last words of the text actually reproduce the traditional blessing offered by Greek oracles to their clients, as we know from a crowd of literary and epigraphic examples.

So too in the more prolix Aramaic version which follows. Here in the language of Persian officialdom are, with slight but significant variations, the same expressions of charity and compassion, this time tempered not to the Greek but to the Iranian mind; as Dupont-Sommer remarks, a little closer (not unnaturally) than the Greek to the Indian original, but aimed carefully, like all the edicts of Ashoka, at the local understanding. To the Greeks or 'Yonas' he talked like a Greek, to the Persians like a Persian

KANDAHAR:
*duplicate rock-cut
inscription in Greek and
Aramaic, c. 255 BC*

administrator of the old régime whose *lingua franca* still endured in a land
of many vernaculars.

In one way and another, the two simultaneous documents on this rocky
outcrop at Kandahar illustrate with a dramatic vividness the multiple elements in the culture of the region three-quarters of a century after
Alexander: the Greek with its continuing social primacy, its Hellenism
still substantially intact, albeit in a remote environment and in confrontation with a powerful alien philosophy; the Persian, beneath the Greek but
hardly proclaiming its own sense of style and tradition; and, from the
background, India with its assertive but beneficent doctrinal ethic, the
first of its catholic kind known to history. The traditional opposition between 'Greek' and 'foreign' or 'barbarian' is on the way out. In its place, no
doubt in this instance encouraged by the political pressures of the strong
Mauryan régime, we face the beginnings of a new cultural fusion on an

international scale. The general picture is that of one of the happier and more intelligent moments of human and humane interchange.

But that is not the whole of the story. In 1963 an inscribed rectangular building-stone was recovered from debris in Old Kandahar, though what the debris represented could not be ascertained (pages 60–1). The face of the stone is covered by a Greek epigraph consisting of twenty-two long lines, incomplete in all four directions but sufficient to indicate that they were again a paraphrase and modification of a part of Ashoka's fourteen Major Rock Edicts; more precisely, of the twelfth and thirteenth. The paraphrase had doubtless occupied the surface of some public building but whether, like the rock-inscription of 1958, it had been accompanied by an Aramaic version there is no evidence. In translation the inscription reads as follows:

. . . piety and self-mastery in all the schools of thought; and he who is master of his tongue is most master of himself. And let them neither praise themselves nor disparage their neighbours in any matter whatsoever, for that is vain. In acting in accordance with this principle they exalt themselves and win their neighbours; in transgressing in these things they misdemean themselves and antagonize their neighbours. Those who praise themselves and denigrate their neighbours are self-seekers, wishing to shine in comparison with the others but in fact hurting themselves. It behoves to respect one another and to accept one another's lessons. In all actions it behoves to be understanding, sharing with one another all that each one comprehends. And to those who strive thus let there be no hesitation to say these things in order that they may persist in piety in everything.

In the eighth year of the reign of Piodasses, he conquered Kalinga. A hundred and fifty thousand persons were captured and deported, and a hundred thousand others were killed, and almost as many died otherwise. Thereafter, pity and compassion seized him and he suffered grievously. In the same manner wherewith he ordered abstention from living things, he has displayed zeal and effort to promote piety. And at the same time the king has viewed this with displeasure: of the Brahmins and Sramins and others practising piety who live there [in Kalinga] – and these must be mindful of the interests of the king and must revere and respect their teacher, their father and their mother and love and faithfully cherish their friends and companions and must use their slaves and dependents as gently as possible – if, of those thus engaged there, any has died or been deported and the rest have regarded this lightly, the king has taken it with exceeding bad grace. And that amongst other people there are. . . .

The fragment began, as has been seen, with an incomplete reference to *schools* of thought, using the word *diatribe* which to a Greek signified a 'school of philosophy'. Its precise connotation in Ashoka's Buddhism is conjectural, but, like much else in these two Greek inscriptions, the word must have had a homely sound to Greek ears. The text goes on to denounce self-praise and denigration of others, and to advocate mutual respect. All this comes over well in the Greek, for all that its emphatic morality is rooted in Hindu introspection.

Then Ashoka (Piodasses) goes on to lament almost masochistically the slaughter and misery brought about by his famous campaigns in eastern India against the Kalingas – the primary cause of his conversion to Buddhism. From that moment, pity and compassion had seized upon him, culminating in the vegetarianism which comes readily to the Indian way of life. The main theme is accompanied by a catalogue of virtues which include respect for master and parents and an injunction to 'use slaves and dependents as gently as possible' (this last an interesting anticipation of the humanitarianism which, in the West, scarcely emerged until the end of the Roman Republic). In all this we are in the Orient of the third century BC, but the Greek adapter has done his best to acclimatize Indian sentiment to Greek idiom.

Indeed, once again it is the 'Greekness' of the text that strikes the reader. As Louis Robert has pointed out in discussion, the sustained cultural unity of the far-flung Hellenistic world in the third century BC is an astonishing phenomenon. These inscriptions from the depths of Asia, although marking the advent of new and oriental ideas, show no hint of degeneration or provincialism in expression. Their style runs free, with a certain iteration for emphasis and leisurely popular consumption but with a tightness of phraseology in the concise Greek manner. Their vocabulary is wholly borrowed from the Greek literary and philosophical tradition. There is nothing laboured in its rendering of the Indian prototype.

We need then no longer hesitate to accept a full-blown 'Alexandria' upon the site of Old Kandahar. This was no mere tired vestige of a passing army. It was a balanced Greek city with its writers, its philosophers, its teachers, no less than its executives and its growing environment of Hellenized 'natives', who may have been the Kambojas mentioned in that same thirteenth Edict. The original name 'Alexandria' may not here have survived

KANDAHAR: rock-cut Greek inscription of c. 255 BC, found in 1958. (Cf. p. 67)

the Seleucid successors of the conqueror. The rechristening of Alexander's foundations by later potentates was a not-uncommon vanity, and Alexandria in Arachosia may be identical with the Demetrias in Arachosia recorded by the geographer Isidore of Charax in the first century BC from earlier authority. By the first century AD the city seems to have been content with the unqualified name of its province, Arachosia (Pliny, VI, 92); but Bactra itself, capital of the Bactrian kingdom, and Termez across the Oxus were no less prodigal of their royal ancestry. All this was a matter of fashion and favour, not of fact.

We turn to witness of another kind. Save on the masterly coins of the Bactrian and Indian Greeks, the Kandahar epigraphs were until 1965 the only significant material evidence in any form of Alexander's transit east of Persepolis. The most important historical site – the primary centre of eastern Hellenism – was Bactra itself, on the northern flank of the Hindu Kush and in the once-fertile plain of what is now the steppe of Afghan

Turkestan beside a dried-up tributary of the Oxus. This provincial capital of Achaemenid times was refounded or duplicated by Alexander as another Alexandria. Today the famous city, which in or about 208 BC withstood Antiochus III for no less than two years, is represented by the little town of Balkh and an accumulative circuit of some seven miles of dusty heaps, with a high acropolis in their midst. It has never been adequately excavated, and its presumed Greek strata have never been uncovered, though occasionally Hellenistic objects have been identified. Pottery of a similar period seems to occur at Shar-i-Banu, on the Oxus plain north of Tashkurgān. More important, some forty miles to the north of Balkh, on the opposite bank of the Oxus, rise the lofty mounds of what seems to be yet another Alexandria, founded upon the pre-Alexandrian Tarmata or Tarmita, a name which has re-emerged in the modern Termez. Here Russian archaeologists have been digging for several years, with results as yet imperfectly known. Throughout the region, vagueness or vacuity has prevailed in modern times without serious challenge.

Now suddenly the prospect offers welcome signs of change, and the story, as told by Professor Daniel Schlumberger, is worth re-telling. In 1961 the King of Afghanistan was hunting near the northern border of his kingdom when he was shown two carved stones which he recognized as of an unusual kind. One was the battered capital of a large Corinthian column, the other was a small columnar pedestal or altar. They had been found in the sparsely inhabited vicinity of the village of Aï Khanum ('Lady Moon' in Uzbek), beside the river Oxus at the point where it is joined from the southeast by a tributary, the Kokcha, some forty miles north-east of Kunduz. Later in that year at Kabul the King told Daniel Schlumberger of the discovery, and in 1962 the stones were seen and recorded by the French Archaeological Delegation at Kunduz, whither they had meanwhile been transferred.

So far, so good. The Corinthian capital was the first certain vestige of an all-stone column of classical type ever found up to that date in ancient Bactria. Its size, moreover, showed it to have come from a building of impressive magnitude. The importance of the King's discovery was manifest but, from that point, advance was difficult. The Oxus constitutes the boundary between Afghanistan and the Soviet Union, which here regards its neighbour from commanding cliffs. The exposed region on the Afghan side is understandably a military zone where the prospecting archaeologist is not encouraged.

At the end of 1963, however, high influence at last prevailed, and Schlumberger and his architect, Marc le Berre, were allowed to spend two hours upon the site. In the gathering darkness, its importance was immediately manifest. There under the dust was the ghost of a complete Hellenistic city. A year later, the explorers were, with manifest hesitation but not

75

without diplomatic courage, enabled to return with a tiny staff and to carry out soundings over a period of ten days. This momentary inspection in depth confirmed surmise. Here was a well-preserved and embattled outpost of the Greek world on a scale worthy, not merely of modern royal recognition, but of royal enterprise on the grand scale nearly twenty-three centuries ago. Here at last, it would appear, was the handiwork of Alexander, or, at least, of one of his close successors, sited strategically at the natural north-eastern gateway into Bactria. And subsequent excavation in 1965 and 1966, commanded by Paul Bernard, who assumed the Directorship of the French Delegation on the retirement of Daniel Schlumberger, has amplified the supposition (pages 63, 70 and following).

The general plan of the city is the natural development of a carefully chosen site. It is set within the protective angle formed by the Oxus and its tributary, and falls into two main parts: the upper city or acropolis on

AÏ KHANUM:
*reconstruction of a
Corinthian capital from
the 'agora'. (By P.
Bernard and M. Le
Berre)*

a rocky, earth-covered plateau of roughly triangular shape and nearly a
mile in length; and the lower city, on humus and gravel, extending to the
rivers on the west and south and stretching northwards nearly a thousand
yards beyond the end of the plateau. This northern stretch – the only part
of the plan devoid of natural protection – was defended by a wall with large
and frequent rectangular towers, each some sixty-five feet wide, and fronted
by a ditch, with a central gateway (pages 72–3). The upper town, rising to
a height of some 130 feet above the lower, was also in some measure fortified in spite of its abrupt sides; and its southern end was cut off by a broad
transverse ditch to form a citadel. North of this ditch, the plateau was
further subdivided by two cross-walls, seemingly of lesser importance.
Along the flanks of the upper town are traces of an earth-cut aqueduct
which was fed by the Kokcha at the point where it enters the plain some
nine miles to the south-east.

In the interior of the lower city, a main street traverses the site from the
gateway in the northern fortifications to the bank of the Kokcha in the
south. Here the southern gateway would appear to have been washed
away by the river. Beside the street, to the east, at the foot of the upper city,

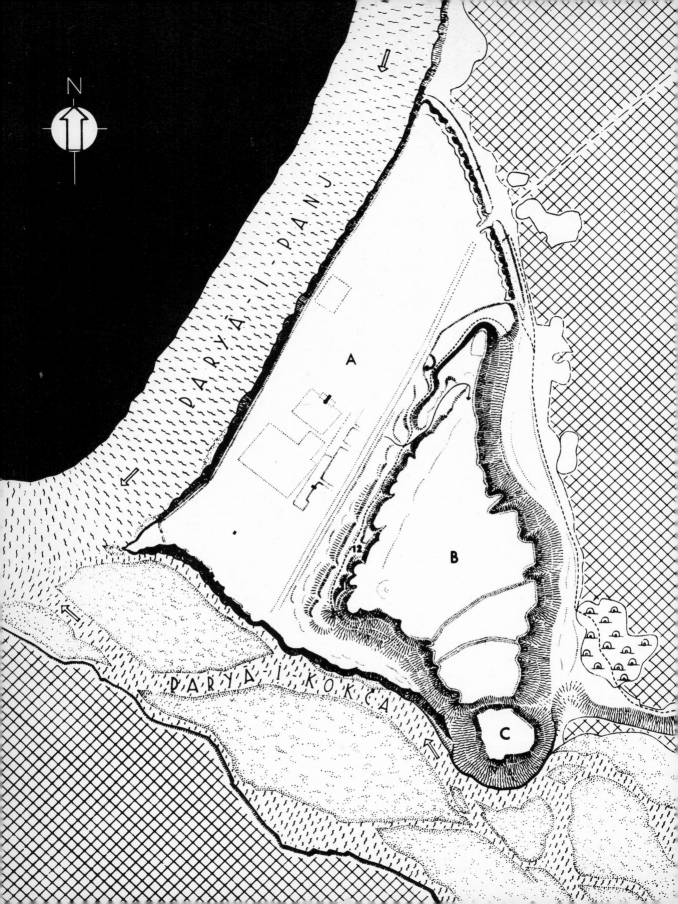

AÏ KHANUM:
*Persian base and
Corinthian capital in
the entry into the
'agora'*

a semicircular hollow has been suspected of marking the position of the theatre. To the west of the street a long depression has been thought to represent the stadium, though this would normally lie outside the fortified area. In the vicinity important mounds mark the position of public buildings. Further south was apparently the principal living-quarter; whilst to the north a seeming absence of permanent habitations may indicate an open area for refugees and their flocks in case of need.

Amongst the public buildings of the lower town, excavation has already revealed the presence of a large rectangular courtyard, 450 by 360 feet, lined with colonnaded porticos of the Corinthian order backed by a brick wall between stone pilasters corresponding with the pillars in front. The courtyard was entered from the north by a monumental gateway, again with Corinthian columns though these have a single thick *torus* or 'bolster' base of a Persian type found, for example, at Persepolis (see above). The portico on the south, towards the prevailing winds, was both deeper and higher than the others, as in the domestic porticos known to Vitruvius as 'Rhodian', and opened on the south into a large hypostyle hall (again possibly a Persian feature) with eighteen Corinthian columns arranged in three rows of six. These columns have typical Attico-Asiatic bases with a hollow moulding (*scotia*) between two convex mouldings (*tori*), whilst the capitals show features comparable with Seleucid types of the second century BC (pages 71, 76, 77). The walls of the courtyard were painted and were further decorated with medallions of unbaked clay in relief representing lions' heads. The roofs were tiled with well-made orange-coloured tiles of terracotta and of a distinctive type which, as Monsieur Bernard has pointed out, resembles that of Hellenistic tiles from Priene, Olbia, Olynthus and elsewhere. Throughout there is an abundant use of bright colours on

AÏ KHANUM:
*plan of the Hellenistic city.
A, Lower City; B, Acropolis;
C, Inner citadel. (The black
area is USSR territory)*

the architectural details – green, yellow, red, black and white; and there are fragments of statues of plastered clay, flesh-coloured. The building was probably the principal *agora* or market-place.

Two further buildings have been wholly or partially investigated, both distinguished by the finding of Greek inscriptions. The first, near the Oxus in the northern part of the city, is another large courtyard-structure which probably represents a gymnasium or *palaestra*: one of those characteristically Greek establishments where the youth of the Hellenic world combined the physical and intellectual training which was comprised by the untranslatable word *paideia*, education in the broadest sense. Appropriately the buildings yielded a dedication to Hermes and Heracles who, as gods of cleverness and muscularity, took a special interest in these institutions.

The other discovery was not less significant. About forty yards north of the very large courtyard first described above was a small temple-like building which is, no doubt correctly, interpreted as a funerary *heroön*, the ceremonial burial-place of some important personage (opposite). This is more likely than not to have been the actual founder of the city or his deputy; just as, for example, the traditional tomb of Battus, who is said to have founded Cyrene in North Africa after consulting the Delphic oracle, was piously preserved in the *agora* or market-place of that great city. Otherwise, a place of burial of this ostentatious kind is very unlikely to have been tolerated within the circuit of a Hellenistic foundation. The hero of Aï Khanum appears to have been an otherwise unknown Kineas, whose name occurs in an inscription, of which more in a moment.

The *heroön* is described as having passed through three structural phases, each retaining with variations the plan of a *cella* or shrine with a *pronaos* or

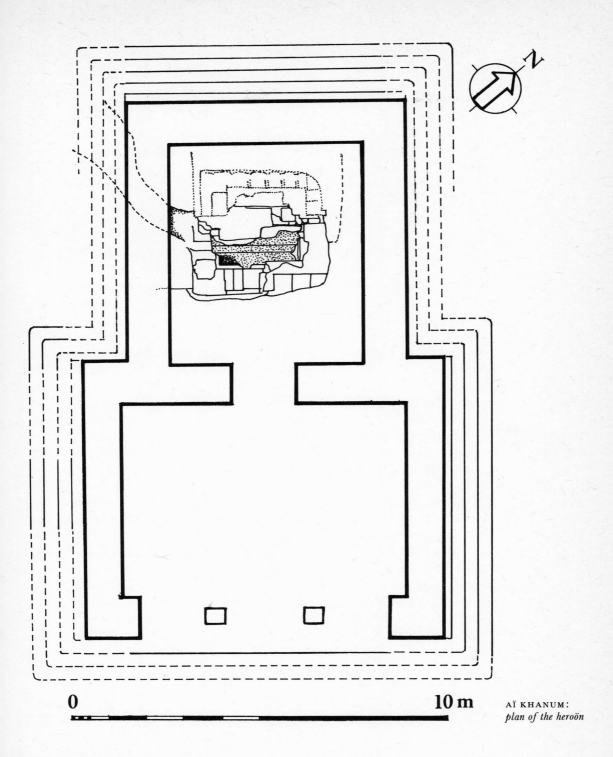

AÏ KHANUM:
plan of the heroön

porch which included two wooden pillars on stone bases and faced east. The original structure stood on a stepped podium, rather like the tomb of Cyrus at Pasargadae in Persia (page 33). Under the successive floors of the *cella* were four burials, two in plain sarcophagi and two in graves lined with baked bricks. All had been robbed except for one of the latter, which contained a skeleton and traces of a wooden coffin but no grave-goods. The lower of the two sarcophagi was presumably the first buried, that of the great man whom the tomb primarily commemorated.

Reset in the *pronaos* of the third and latest period was a stone base provided with a large socket on its upper face and two inscriptions carved side by side, evidently at the same time, on the front face. Epigraphically they are attributed to the third century BC. That on the left is described by Monsieur Bernard as 'a short epigram of two elegiac distichs written in a literary, archaistic language. It states that one Klearchos had had transcribed, in the *temenos* of Kineas, certain precepts that had been dedicated in the holy Pytho, that is to say Delphi, where he (Klearchos) had copied them.' The stela on which most of the Delphic precepts were engraved has disappeared, but these had overflowed on to the pedestal, so that the last one is cut in monumental lettering beside the epigram. It is part of a series of Delphic maxims exhorting the acquisition of the fundamental qualities of man at each stage of his life. In fact the maxims are known to us from literary sources and from an epigraphic copy found at Miletopolis in Anatolia. As Bernard observes, 'their presence on the banks of the Oxus, more than five thousand kilometres as the crow flies from Delphi, is an astonishing testimony to the fidelity of these Greek settlers of remote Bactria to the most authentic and venerable traditions of Hellenism'. The oracular undertone already noted in one of the Greek inscriptions from Kandahar is here even more explicit and emphatic.

In the same *pronaos* was discovered the first Graeco-Bactrian sculpture known: a cloaked herm with the bearded head of an old man, with the diadem of a priest or high official (pages 83, 85). The right hand clasps the cloak from underneath, whilst the left hand held a bronze staff now lost. The work is probably a portrait, and is of a satisfactory Hellenistic standard. It may fairly be described as a landmark in Bactrian art, and will be taken into account when we come to the later problems of Gandhara art (page 164).

In one way and another, this city at Aï Khanum is already, in the early stages of its revelation, a human and historical witness of the first order. It was the work of adventurous and imaginative and above all civilized pioneers on the uttermost fringe of the Eurasian world. The ethics of Delphi were here advertized in its midst, probably at the carefully cherished tomb of the founder. The architecture was skilfully sculptured and gaily coloured, in accordance with Western canons though not without occasional acknowledgment of an Eastern environment; here and there

AÏ KHANUM:
*Hellenistic herm
representing an elderly
official*

details such as the bolstered, unclassical base of a column, already referred to, or the winged pseudo-palmette of a roof-ornament have been thought to point to Asian, perhaps Achaemenid influence, as indeed they may. With the progress of discovery, such hybrid elements will no doubt assume a clearer measure of importance. But this will remain secondary to the over-all Hellenism of the scene. Greek priests, philosophers, craftsmen may already be inferred. The stamp on a wine-jar or oil-jar which may be of local manufacture refers to an *agoranomos* or market-controller such as is known in Greek cities of the Black Sea and the Near East. It is not too much to assume that most of the familiar apparatus of Hellenistic urban life will be revealed here in due course.

Two basic and probably related matters for the moment elude us: when was the city founded, and what was its name? Was Aï Khanum in fact one of Alexander's Alexandrias? If so, then it must originally have borne his name, whatever its later vicissitudes. Monsieur Bernard likes to think of it as Ptolemy's Alexandria-on-the-Oxus, thus robbing Termez of the similar claim made for it by Tarn. He may be right, but at present there seems to be no material evidence for the city's existence as early as the fourth century BC. If the Delphic inscription is rightly attributed to the earlier half of the third century BC, then it may be supposed that the leader of the foundation-mission, the Kineas of the inscription, may have acted on behalf of Seleucus I (312–281 BC) or his successor Antiochus I (281–261 BC) who took over the Asian territories of the conqueror. Under these kings Bactria was a satrapy or province of the Seleucid kingdom and was ruled, at least nominally, first from Seleucia on the Tigris and later from the new capital at Antioch in Syria. But the remote province beside the Oxus was in these circumstances very much out on a limb, and it may be questioned whether in the three-quarters of a century after the death of Alexander there lingered in Bactria the surviving will to found a new city of the size and quality of Aï Khanum, however strategic its position. For this, some new stimulus may be thought to have been necessary, and it is not in fact difficult to find one in the tidal history of the period.

In the third quarter of the third century BC, the Bactrian governor Diodotus II or his successor Euthydemus unilaterally declared independence and assumed the royal title. The satrapy of Bactria had become the kingdom of Bactria, and little could be done about it. The moment was ripe for the establishment there of a new instrument or symbol of the new authority, and uncertain tribal movements across the Oxus may have offered an additional inducement. The new city fits into the picture but its name, whatever it may have been, was in that event certainly not Alexandria. It might have been a Euthydemia, but there is as yet no evidence.

In this risky game of guesswork there is one further possibility if, for the moment, we are prepared to waive the third-century date attributed

AÏ KHANUM:
*head of the Hellenistic
herm*

85

provisionally to the Kineas inscription. We have seen how in that century most of India and southern Afghanistan (certainly as far as Kandahar) lay under the strong hand of the great Mauryan emperor Ashoka. But in the accepted year 184 BC the Mauryan dynasty came to an end, and during the subsequent uncertainties King Demetrius of Bactria – an adventurous mind in the Alexander tradition – seized the opportunity to cross the Hindu Kush and to 'occupy' north-western India. In so doing he was reclaiming and expanding the territories traversed by Alexander in 326 but subsequently ceded to the Mauryans by his successor. Further reference will be made to this exploit; for the moment the important issue is that the excursus of Demetrius and his principal colleagues into India had weakened Bactria and tempted intervention by the legitimate power far away at Antioch.

Very briefly, what seems to have happened was somewhat as follows. Antiochus IV, a strange and elusive character but a man of ambition, evidently had it in his mind to re-integrate the old Asian 'empire' of Alexander and his successor Seleucus I, in so far as the agreed frontier with India in the east and the advancing frontiers of Rome in the west allowed. For this purpose, in or about 169 BC he sent his cousin Eucratides to reclaim the territories of the dissident Bactrian kings. Demetrius hastened back from India to meet him, and was killed; Eucratides was in command of Bactria. It may be that Antiochus had already granted him a title equivalent to 'sub-king', by virtue of which he founded or refounded somewhere in Bactria a city bearing his own name, Eucratideia, recorded by Strabo (XI. 516) and Ptolemy (VI. 11, 8). This may of course have been Bactra itself in new guise, or perhaps rather Alexander's Tarmata, which seems to have become one of the name-cities of Demetrius as Demetrias and would now appropriately have been again rechristened by Eucratides; but (and this is pure speculation) Eucratideia may equally have been this newly discovered and majestic city of Aï Khanum which, in view of the seemingly modest depth of its occupation-material, may have been a relatively late foundation rather than a creation either of Alexander or of Euthydemus. But be it repeated that this becomes less than a guess if the epigraphists decide to adhere with good reason to the provisional third-century dating of the Kineas inscription.

In any case, this recently found, remote Hellenistic city may be expected to contribute new evidence towards the solution of a notorious problem in the history of art: how and whence did the vastly productive Buddhist school of Gandhara – the north-western frontier region of Indo-Pakistan – receive in the early centuries AD the Greek or Graeco-Roman elements which are manifest and familiar in its composition? Old theory derived them from Greek Bactria; but as years went by without evidence of any Hellenistic sculptural art in Bactria, other sources were desperately sought.

In particular the unquestionably Roman trade which came this way in the first and second centuries AD has been regarded as an alternative intermediary. It may be that the excavators of Aï Khanum have the true answer beneath their feet. After all, the road from Persepolis may have brought more than politics and princes to the further east.

AFTER THE BURNING: 2

INDO-GREEK CITIES

previous page
CHARSADA
(*Pushkalavati*) : *the*
primary city-mound or
Bala Hisar from the
south

TAXILA
(*Bhir Mound*):
impressions of Graeco-
Persian seals of
c. 300 BC,
with impressions

Whatever the upshot of the exploration of Aï Khanum – and if it can be carried to any sort of conclusion it is certain to be vivid and various – there is no doubt as to the debt which certain towns across the Hindu Kush, in the southern fringe of Afghanistan and the north-west of Indo-Pakistan, owed to the descendants of Alexander's Greeks. Here archaeology has been more attentive and successful than, until very recently, in the Bactrian homeland. The circumstances are briefly these.

From Bactria in 327 BC the Macedonian armies thrust through the mountains to the southern fringe of the Hindu Kush (the *Paropamisadae* of the classical geographers) where, fifty miles north of Kabul and three miles to the north-east of the modern town of Charikar, three routes through the range converged beside the Panjshir-Ghorband rivers. Here, at the present Begram, stood the ancient Kapisi, a local capital, and, there or close by, another Alexandria – 'Alexandria-of-the-Caucasus' – was now established (pages 108–9).

The site of Alexander's foundation has not been identified. There is no evidence at present that it occupied the actual site of Kapisi; equally, there is no conclusive evidence that it did not. The French archaeologists who dug here for several years made remarkable discoveries but did not penetrate analytically in depth, and even the general topography is far from clear. On the broad lines proposed by R. Ghirshman, however, who continued the work under admittedly harassing conditions in 1941–2, the considerable vestiges are provisionally interpreted as follows (page 92).

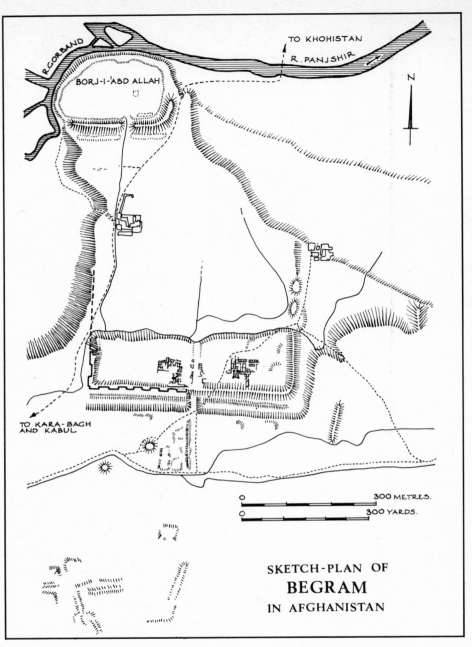

SKETCH-PLAN OF
BEGRAM
IN AFGHANISTAN

At the junction of the rivers Panjshir and Ghorband which emerge from
the high mountains to the north, a rocky steep-sided promontory known as
the Bordj-i'Abdullah projects into the multiple streams. At some uncertain
date the summit of the promontory was turned into a fortress or small
fortified town by the construction of a sturdy wall and ditch on the southern

and part of the eastern sides, which are not naturally protected. The area thus enclosed was roughly three hundred yards from east to west and a hundred and sixty yards from north to south. There was an entrance near the centre of the southern side.

The top of the promontory has been considerably scraped and confused by cultivation, but Ghirshman's cutting across the defensive wall showed that it had been as much as forty-three feet wide, built of earth and rubble revetted fore and aft by vertical walls of mud-brick, each eight feet wide. Towards the interior it was enlarged by a revetted ledge or low peripheral walk about ten feet wide. No wall-towers were identified, and the ditch was not sectioned. Being at the naturally defensible end of the promontory, this fortress was presumably established prior to the development of the flat area to the south, but no material evidence of its date has yet been recovered. It may go back, as a small military post or colony, to the time of Alexander or even to that of his predecessors, the Achaemenid Persians. Buildings in the interior have not been found, nor indeed adequately sought.

A little more can be said of the impressive fortifications which have been partially cleared on the level ground six hundred and fifty yards further south. Hereabouts both Ghirshman and his predecessor Hackin concentrated their major efforts. The defences consist of a straight wall some five hundred and fifty yards from east to west, turning northwards at a right-angle at each end. Rectangular bastions, each some fifty-five feet wide, project at frequent and equal intervals, with a central gateway (of unascertained plan) approached from the south by a causeway across a broad double ditch. The wall is thirty-three feet wide and consists of a central filling (thought to be a 'passage') between two vertical revetments of mud-brick upon stone foundations. Between the two ditches and beyond the outer one, auxiliary ramparts have been suspected but not examined.

The general aspect of the wall with its close-set towers recalls that of Aï Khanum, which is not closely dated at the time of writing. It is also partially comparable, in anticipation, with that of Taxila-Sirkap (see below), where the stone-bastioned defences probably date from the first century BC and may be the work of Indo-Greeks or Hellenizing Scythians. At Begram, Hackin and Ghirshman partially cleared a number of buildings within the lines of the walls; and Ghirshman recognized three successive periods, of which the earliest was equated with coins of Eucratides, Menander, Hermaios and 'other Graeco-Bactrian kings' (*sic*) – roughly 167–50 BC. But the evidence altogether lacks precision. It does not help to accept the supposition (likely enough in itself) that coins struck a century and a half after Alexander by Pantaleon and Agathocles, sons of the Demetrius mentioned above, may have been minted hereabouts because they show a seated Zeus holding a three-headed Hecate, 'Hecate of the

Three Ways', such as would be appropriate to this important triple road-junction. Begram needs fresh digging by modern methods, and the whole region demands fresh exploration.

Within the southern defences a main street proceeded in a straight line northwards from the central gateway and there are hints that it formed the backbone of a rectilinear street-plan of normal Hellenistic type. So far as excavated, the street was flanked on both sides by shops, beyond which lay more extensive houses and public buildings constructed in mud-brick, sometimes based on stone. These various structures mostly began in Ghirshman's Phase I, which he extends from the Graeco-Bactrians through subsequent Scytho-Parthians until the arrival of the Kushan dynasty from central Asia *via* Turkestan and eastern Iran in the latter part of the first century AD. Under the Kushans of Phase II the town continued with modifications until it was destroyed by the invading Sassanid Persians in the third century AD, whereafter it was built substantially afresh (Phase III) within the old fortifications. With these later phases we are not here concerned.

So far as can be seen at present therefore, and pending further investigation, there is a likelihood that Begram assumed something like its surviving outline in the second century BC, when Greeks from Bactria were increasingly interested in the re-occupation and redevelopment of north-western India. It is probable enough that about the middle of the century the great Menander himself had a hand in the business. Of the preceding transit of Alexander it is scarcely surprising that material evidence is hard to come by. Indeed, up to the present only at one spot – a hundred and sixty miles south-east of Begram – has archaeology claimed a visual vestige of his passing.

It should be premised that, on emerging from the Hindu Kush, Alexander's troops were following a well-trodden highway of the former Achaemenid traffic-system. Along this highway, which ultimately reached the Ganges, a series of native principalities had established or developed their local authority, trading and taxing in an uneasy and competitive fashion. What political and geographical relationships these principalities had with the official provinces or satrapies established two centuries previously by Cyrus and the first Darius at the time of the Persian conquest of north-western India is not clear. It is to be presumed that in practice the native governors or kinglets in this far-off extremity of the Persian Empire had gradually assumed most of the *de facto* control, retaining little more than formal liaison, if that, with their imperial masters. No doubt in their own interests they maintained a measure of discipline along the imperial traffic-routes, thus ensuring in return a rake-off from the passing caravans; and in the declining days of Achaemenid power this arrangement may have worked as well as any other. At any rate, such appears to have been the situation when Alexander appeared upon the scene. He encountered no remaining substance of Persian dominion in the old Persian territories south-east of the Hindu Kush.

His advance from the mountains into the province of Gandhara – essentially the plain of Peshawar – was both discursive and adventurous, and is still good schoolboy-reading. In the present context only one of its incidents is relevant. While Alexander himself made a detour through the northern hills, a formidable division of his troops was sent under the command of his trusted Hephaestion to clear the plain of opposition and to prepare the further advance across the Indus.

Here, in the midst of Gandhara, Hephaestion's main objective was the province known to the Greeks as Peukelaotis, with Peukela as its provincial capital. The Sanskrit name for the city was Pushkalavati, the 'City of Lotuses'; and the lotus-flower is both stamped upon some of its pottery and seems to be carried by the city-goddess on a unique gold coin in the British Museum. The impressive mounds which today tower above the plain on the outskirts of the town of Charsada, twenty miles north-east of Peshawar and near the junction of the rivers Swat and Kabul, were identified with the ancient city over a century ago by the infallible Alexander Cunningham, and the identification is not disputed (pages 88–9 and below).

The scene presented by these dusty mounds is no ordinary one. The horizon, when the mists withdraw, is lined towards the north by the mountains amidst which the Malakand Pass climbs arduously beside the river Swat to the fort-capped highlands of Swat and Dir. Towards the west the Kabul valley breaks through the hills which flank the busy Khyber Pass. In the foreground the plain is a sea of virid sugar-crops, varied by the yellow, sandy islands which represent Pushkalavati in its changing manifestations. Amongst them the tallest mound, and no doubt the most ancient, is known as the Bala Hisar, the High Fort, and is upwards of fifty feet high;

CHARSADA (*Pushkalavati*): *the primary city-mound or Bala Hisar from the south-east*

it rides on the sugar-sea for all the world like an old battleship at anchor. In area it is now considerably less than half its former size. I recall how, on my first visit to the place in 1944, I had to push my way up the narrow approaches through an opposing herd of buffaloes, each carrying a double pannier filled with the valued phosphatic dust of the high mound for use as agricultural top-dressing. The great mound was being, and had long been, systematically undermined and tumbled by the peasantry, and I remember that something approaching a military campaign had to be improvised to stop the assault. Since then, armed guards have ensured the survival of what was left, in a countryside where the rifle is still something more than merely visual authority.

Excavation of a more responsible kind was carried out in and near the Bala Hisar in 1958, and both it and the lower but more extensive mounds in its neighbourhood are beginning to tell a sensible story. It is this. The High Fort first came into existence as a town at ground-level, some fifteen to twenty acres in extent, beside a stream which flowed into one or other of the two adjacent rivers. The date of its birth is conjectural, but iron was already in established use there and, if we may be bold enough to take at face value the plausible statement in the Indian epic *Ramayana* that Push-kalavati and Taxila were founded by two brothers, the sixth century BC is something more than a likely guess, on one side or the other of the absorption of the region into the Persian Empire before 518 BC. In or about that year, Gandhara was already included amongst his possessions by Darius I on his great rock-inscription at Behistun in western Persia, and this central Gandharan town beside the Kabul river, which marked the main highway into India from the north-west, either began or at least quickly developed in response to the new impulse of organized imperial commerce.

Excavation has shown that, by the time of Alexander, Pushkalavati had risen to a height of twelve or thirteen feet – less than a quarter of the present height of the mound – by the processes normal to ancient mud-built cities; each successive phase standing upon the accumulated debris of its earthy predecessors. It was at that time under the governorship of one Astes who, with a spirit not shared by other local Indian rulers, 'caused some trouble' on the advent of the invader and had to be tackled in force. In fact we are told (by Arrian) that he held out against a siege of thirty days, and, since Hephaestion's division comprised no less than three brigades of infantry, half of the horse-guards and the whole of the mercenary cavalry, the beleaguered town must have been substantially fortified. During our excavations of 1958 these defences were sought and found below the present surface to the east of the high mound, following the western bank of the former stream. Whether the stream was itself artificially incorporated in the system as a semi-natural fosse was not ascertained (it was not cross-trenched); but along its margin a v-shaped ditch was

identified for a distance of three hundred and twenty yards, together with the site of an earthen rampart originally faced externally, it seems, by a wall of mud-brick four feet wide. At the central point the post-holes of a timber-lined postern and bridge were uncovered (see above).

A further detail of some interest was revealed by the excavation. From top to bottom the ditch had been refilled with clean earth containing here and there fallen mud-bricks. At its lowest point there was a mere handful of the in-wash known to archaeologists as 'rapid silt'. The inference is clear: the ditch had been open for a very short time. And since the marginal stream on the one side and the remains of the town on the other preclude any alternative site for the fortifications of the Alexander-episode, the synchronization of this ditch and rampart with Hephaestion's siege is certain; whilst it is equally certain that they were hastily constructed on the approach of the Macedonian invader and that they were destroyed (by throwing the rampart back into the ditch) when the town was 'slighted' upon its capture. Their ruin is a monument to the resolute but futile independence of Astes, who, as the reliable Arrian tells us, 'lost his life in the process and involved in his own ruin the town in which he had attempted to hold out'.

CHARSADA (*Pushkalavati*): *defensive ditch round the Bala Hisar and, on right, site of rampart, erected against Alexander in 327 B.C. The post-holes indicate a postern and bridge*

The event was an important one and Alexander, though we can only guess the tactical intent of his manoeuvres, seems to have come out of his way to accept the surrender of Pushkalavati in proper form. Whilst Hephaestion had been clearing the plain, his chief had been campaigning in the Swat highlands. Now, before re-entering the hills to storm Aornos – a mountain stronghold that had baffled Heracles himself! – he descended to the captured city, took it over (no doubt with suitable showmanship) and 'garrisoned it with Macedonian troops under the command of Philip' – probably, though not certainly, the same semi-royal Philip who afterwards took over the immense satrapy of north-western India and was eventually murdered.

Little is known at present of the internal aspect of the Pushkalavati which Alexander's Hephaestion brought to ruin, though something of its general character may fairly be inferred by anticipating the witness of Taxila, to which we shall shortly come. It was, on analogy, an untidy place, untidy in its planning and slum-like in the density of its population. For a time, no doubt, the Macedonian garrison was content to camp out in improvized fashion; and the place probably vanished completely as a power when Alexander organized his Indian satrapies before turning homeward in the summer of 326 BC. It was not yet the moment for the methodical rehabilitation of the occupied cities on the Indian side of the Hindu Kush.

But that moment came in the fulness of time. It came when, a century and a half after Alexander's death, about 180 BC, the Demetrius whom we have already encountered (p. 86) forced the Hindu Kush from Bactria and initiated the re-colonization of Alexander's Indian satrapies. This process gave a new shape to the civilization of the north-western quarter of the subcontinent; brought to it a new discipline and a new zest. Now at last the fleeting shadow of Alexander's almost phantom army assumed 'the substance of things hoped for'. Possibly, as we have seen, at Begram (Kapisi), so more certainly at Pushkalavati this involved nothing less than the transfer of the town to a new, clean site where inherited casualness and opportunism could be forgotten and the Hellenistic mode introduced without eviction or other embarrassment. A similar urban revolution will be encountered again at Taxila; and beyond the present context the notorious inconstancy of the proliferating city of Delhi illustrates in later ages the continuing extent to which, on the Indian scene, changes of fashion or of dynasty have been liable to demand the prestige and comfort of fresh ground and uninhibited re-planning.

At Pushkalavati something of this secular vacillation was demonstrated in a simple and very modern way.

Nowadays it is the common custom of archaeologists, whenever circumstance permits, to observe or photograph their chosen subject from the air.

When the light is right, when the ground is suitably dry (or damp) to encourage differential plant-growth or soil-coloration, air-photography can be a blessed ally in the preliminary detection of buried or unemphatic features. Sometimes a bird's-eye vista will help merely by assembling coherently a number of superficial evidences which mean little when viewed in detail at close and myopic range. And this last process wrought something of a marvel at Pushkalavati. On the first day of my season's work there in 1958, the Pakistan Air Force generously sent a jet-plane with a camera to the complex and fragmented site and, in a series of swoops lasting in all about a dozen minutes, photographed the whole area in detail, over a mile square, with revealing and astonishing results. Amongst them, one is outstanding.

It has already been indicated that the site today consists of a series of more or less disconnected sandy mounds, of which the Bala Hisar is merely the most upstanding (pages 88–9, 95). Soundings carried out in 1903 in two of the more easterly of these mounds, suggested occupation during the Kushana periods of the early centuries AD; but one of them, known as

CHARSADA (*Pushkalavati*): *view from the summit of the primary city-mound or Bala Hisar. The long, low mound in the middle distance beyond the sugar-crops is Shaikhan, the site of the Indo-Greek city founded about 150 BC*

99

Shaikhan Dheri, some six hundred yards north of the Bala Hisar, remained unsampled. The air-photographs of 1958 suddenly and vividly demonstrated its significance. It represents an Indo-Greek city with the characteristically Hellenistic features of its kind (opposite).

The Shaikhan mound, now bitten round the edges, still extends to half-a-mile in length upon the western side of the river Swat. Towards the river it carries a few farm-houses and cottages and a spreading Muslim grave-yard. For the rest, as one walks over the site any general comprehension is frustrated by a tumult of heaps and hollows marking the spots where the local villagers have dug up ancient brick walls for the re-use of their material. Not until air-photography integrated these disturbances did they fall into meaningful shape; but then the meaning was not for an instant in doubt. The simple and convincing picture was that of a grid-plan, with a series of parallel streets – not less than five can be identified – mostly forty yards apart and flanked by intelligible house-plans. One interval, as wide as fifty yards, includes the wreck of a circular *stupa* (a Buddhist or, less probably, Jaina shrine), set in an oblong courtyard. Like all the other buildings shown in this notable air-photograph, it is in negative, represented solely by the spoil-trenches dug by the village plunderers, on the principle of 'find a wall and follow it and pull it out'.

During their depredations the brick-hunters are known to have brought to light at least two coin-hoards which included fifteen of Menander (Graeco-Buddhist king of north-western India, about 160–140 BC) and extended to Hermaios about a century later. In 1963 and 1964 Professor A. H. Dani of Peshawar University directed careful soundings of the site and his University has published the results in *Ancient Pakistan* II. The main points are these.

In the river pebbles on the natural surface of the site he found square copper coins of the Indo-Greeks Agathocles and Apollodotus, of whom little can be said save that they were seemingly near-predecessors of Menander and may be ascribed to the second quarter of the second century BC. Consistently, the first structural floor produced a square copper of Menander himself; and Professor Dani is no doubt right in ascribing the foundation of the city substantially to this greatest of Indo-Greek rulers, towards the middle of the century. Other Indo-Greek coins included issues of Antialkidas, whose name will recur in the next chapter, Heliocles, Lysias, Telephus and Philoxenus. From the same Hellenistic level came a little terracotta *putto* of purely Classical type (page 102). The sub-Greek city is well and truly established.

At the same time Professor Dani's soundings showed that, amidst reconstructions and additions in detail, the original street-grid of the place remained undisturbed until the city was removed to an adjacent site under the Kushana king Vashudeva I, somewhere about the beginning of the

CHARSADA
(*Pushkalávati*):
*ancient impression of
a Hellenistic seal
showing Pallas Athene*

left
CHARSADA
(*Pushkalavati*):
*alabaster statuette of
Heracles, or possibly
Alexander. Found with
material of the 2nd
century* BC

right
CHARSADA
(*Pushkalavati*):
terracotta putto
*holding a bird. Found
in the Indo-Greek level
of Shaikhan*

third century AD. Meanwhile it had passed successively through the hands of Scythians, Parthians and the earlier Kushanas, seemingly without material interruption. It may be added, in anticipation of chapter VII, that there was no hint of 'Gandhara art' until the second century AD.

Now in the path of Alexander we leave Pushkalavati and, following the old Persian highway across the Indus, reach the famous city of Taxila some forty miles beyond. Taxila was the capital of a kingdom or principality which lay approximately midway between the Indus and the Jhelum, and the approach of the invader gave its king a chance of enlisting foreign aid against a troublesome neighbour. The king's son, Ambhi, a young man of considerable foresight aided by an efficient intelligence service, had already opened negotiations with Alexander beyond the Indus and, on succeeding his father shortly afterwards, received the invader with every sort of ingratiating courtesy. At the crossing of the Indus, where the good

Hephaestion and his advance-party had prepared a bridge and collected boats and two thirty-oared galleys, a contingent of cavalry from Taxila waited to join Alexander's forces, together with two hundred talents of silver, three thousand oxen, over ten thousand sheep and some thirty elephants. In accordance with custom, Alexander forthwith offered sacrifice to his gods and held a contest of athletics and horsemanship beside the river. The omens from the sacrifice were favourable for the crossing, and in due course there were more games and sacrifices at Taxila itself where, escorted by the king, he held a durbar.

Upwards of twenty years of excavation by Sir John Marshall and his colleagues during the early part of this century have revealed something of the Taxila which greeted the new overlord (page 104). The life of the town doubtless entertained his receptive mind and is recorded by his staff-chroniclers, but its general aspect cannot have impressed him. Outside the gates, a cloud of whistling kites and brooding vultures marked the ground

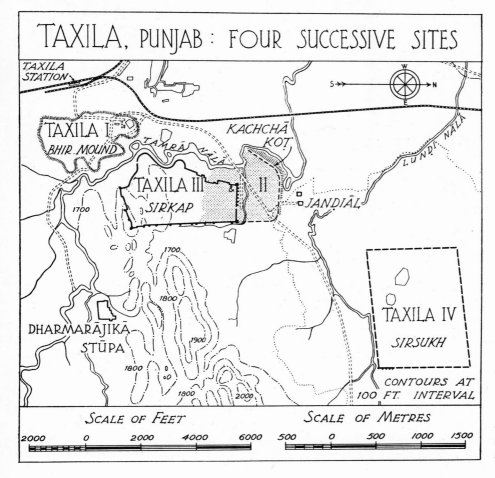

TAXILA:
map of the successive cities

where, in the Persian manner, the dead were exposed for excarnation. Nearby was the spot where, as he was told, *sati* or widow-sacrifice took place. The ill-paved streets through which he was escorted were winding and of uncertain width, with irregular encroachment which had completely blocked some of the side-lanes. To Alexander, with the trimness of his own Greek cities in his mind, the scene must have suggested a slum rather than a metropolis. The haphazardness of the streets was reflected in the shoddy planning and building of the shops and houses. The ramshackle walls were of unsquared random blocks of limestone with an infilling of stone fragments and mud, or were occasionally of mud-brick. Here and there they were coated with mud, and through an open door

could sometimes be seen an inner wall with a surface of red-painted plaster. Otherwise, of architectural adornment there seems to have been none. The warren of contiguous rooms and shops was lighted from point to point by small courts or light-wells. One house, somewhat larger than the rest, was grouped more formally round a square courtyard, and one of its ranges consisted of a relatively imposing hall, its roof supported on three great posts which stood upon pedestals of masonry along the main axis. Only at the centre of the city (as revealed by unpublished excavation, above) was there an administrative building of more pretension, placed like an island in the midst of the main street: a large structure with an irregular apsidal end and a substantial cross-hall with wooden roof-supports similar

TAXILA:
part of the earliest city, visited by Alexander, as seen under excavation in 1944. To the left is a crudely built apsidal structure on the line of the central street (unpublished)

to those just mentioned. An occasional post of this kind could also be seen in the lesser houses, always on a pedestal of rubble-masonry.

In the market-place, if archaeology is a fair witness, few save the most local wares were exposed. But in one quarter of it, Alexander observed a throng of girls herded together and twittering, no doubt, like anxious sparrows. He was told that they were of parents too poor to supply the necessary wedding-dowry and that they were therefore for sale, in accordance with an ancient custom not without parallel in more modern times.

His host proceeded, a little rapidly perhaps, to tell him of certain philosophers who resided in a more honourable poverty within the environs. Alexander, prepared for all emergencies, summoned his own staff-philosopher, Onesikritos the Cynic and casual scientist, and bade him bring the sages to the Presence. Onesikritos went off on his mission, and a circumstantial account of the ensuing episode has come down to us. His reception by the sages was chilly enough. He was told by one of them scornfully to remove his clothes (as Indian holy men they were probably themselves naked) and approach in proper humility. Another asked bluntly, 'Why has Alexander come all the way hither?' with the implication that he certainly had not been invited. Thus was Onesikritos summarily dismissed. The king of Taxila himself then intervened, and eventually one of the sages was persuaded to approach Alexander, to whom he proceeded to read a similar lesson. He threw down on the ground a dry and shrivelled hide and planted his foot on the edge of it. But when it was trodden down in one place, it started up everywhere else. He then walked all round the edge of it and showed that the same thing took place wherever he trod; until at length he stepped into the middle, and by so doing made it all lie flat. This parable was intended to show Alexander that he should control his empire from the centre, and not wander away to its extremities, such as Taxila. In one way and another, the proud Westerner got little change out of the wise men of the Punjab.

These and other pleasantries enliven the tradition of the royal occasion. But we also have more tangible results of it. Prior to the advent of Alexander, the cultural equipment of Taxila had been, like its architecture, of an undistinguished order. Now arrived an army bearing the plunder of Asia in its knapsack; and on its heels, as we shall see anon, came the refugee-craftsmen of the broken Persian Empire, seeking new patronage in the golden East. It is no accident that in the Taxila of Alexander's time and the ensuing age we first find evidence of wealth and sophisticated craftsmanship. In a house by which the conqueror himself may have passed, archaeologists have found a pot containing no fewer than 1,167 coins of silver with several pieces of gold and silver jewellery. Amongst the coins, mostly of a local oblong or 'bent bar' type, were a Persian *siglos* showing the Great King careering across his empire with spear and bow, two of

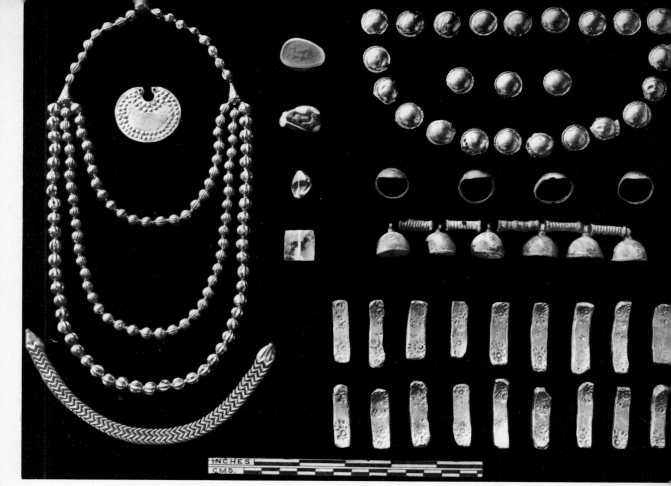

TAXILA:
*hoard of gold and silver jewellery, seal-stones,
and silver 'bent bar' coinage found on the Bhir Mound
in 1945. Date, c. 300 BC* (Taxila Museum)

Alexander the Great, and one of Philip Aridaeus of about 317 BC. Other silver 'bent bar' coins of the same kind were included in another hoard from the same stratum, with gold and silver beads and pendants and two beautiful Graeco-Persian gems, each showing a lion killing a stag (page 91 and above). These hoards and other trifles like them were the accompaniment or aftermath of the episode of 326 BC.

But one innovation had yet to wait its time. When in due course the invading army passed upon its busy way, nothing was done either then or for many years afterwards to bring the city itself into line with Western ideas. Archaeology has shown that, like Pushkalavati, Taxila retained its ancient aspect until the arrival of the Bactrian Greeks from across the Hindu Kush somewhere about 180 BC. And then, again as at Pushkalavati,

opposite
BEGRAM:
*bronze statuette of the
Graeco-Egyptian god
Harpocrates, 1st–2nd
century* AD
Height 5¼ *ins.*
(Kabul Museum)

the change was a revolutionary one. On a new site some hundreds of yards from the old city, a new and orderly Taxila with a rectilinear street-plan of established Hellenistic type came suddenly into being (see above). Push-kalavati-Shaikhan seemingly found its counterpart in Taxila-Sirkap.

The hint of uncertainty in that last sentence may be amplified without pedantic detail. Today the visitor to Sirkap enters through the northern entrance and finds in front of him the straight and wide main street of the city. East and west of him stretches the northern stone fortification, equally straight, twenty feet broad, and armed with square towers above a continuously projecting podium designed to impede sapping. From the eastern end the wall turns southwards at right-angles, again in a straight line and with rectangular towers at close but varying intervals. Towards the south it climbs the steep and rocky ridge of Hathiāl and bends along it westwards, now adapting its course to the sinuosities of the summit. At the foot it turns again northwards, winding in conformity with the adjacent stream. Near the south-western corner a postern-gate has been identified.

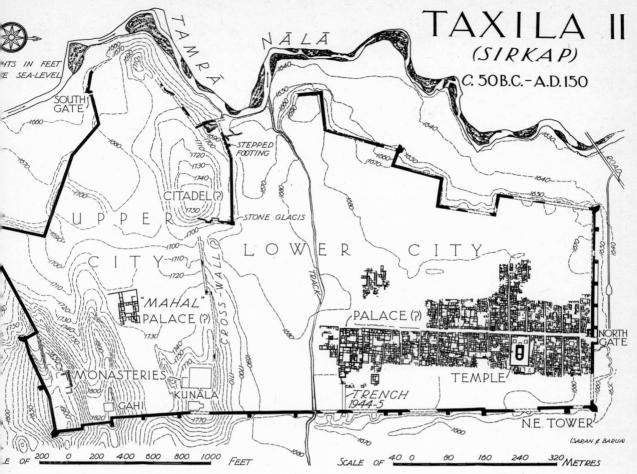

TAXILA II
(SIRKAP)
C. 50 B.C. – A.D. 150

SOUTH GATE

TAMPĀ NĀLĀ

STEPPED FOOTING

CITADEL (?)

STONE GLACIS

U P P E R   C I T Y

L O W E R   C I T Y

CROSS-WALL (?)

TRACK

"MAHAL" PALACE (?)

PALACE (?)

MONASTERIES

KUNĀLA

GAH!

TRENCH 1944-5

TEMPLE

NORTH GATE

N.E. TOWER

ROAD

(SARAN & BARUA)

HTS IN FEET
E SEA-LEVEL

E OF 200 0 200 400 600 800 1000 FEET

SCALE OF 40 0 80 160 240 320 METRES

Within this circuit the street-plan of the lower (northern) part of the city consists, as excavated, of a series of straight narrow lanes spaced at intervals of thirty-five to forty yards and at right-angles to the main street, producing elongated 'islands' or *insulae* crowded with substantial court-yard houses (see above). The flanks of the main street were lined with shops, interrupted here and there by small stupa-shrines and at one place by a large stupa-temple within a compound. Like the stupa-compound at Charsada-Shaikhan, this was fifty yards wide, thus exceeding the normal breadth of the *insulae*. Beside the street, near the centre of the city, a large double-courtyard mansion with a daïs beside each of the courts somewhat anticipates the planning of much later Moghul palaces, and was accordingly identified by the excavator as a royal palace. On the other hand, another large courtyard house known as the Mahal on the slopes of Hathiāl, the acropolis of this period, is more withdrawn from the busy centre and has perhaps a better claim to the royal status which its traditional name ('The Hall') might suggest.

TAXILA:
plan of Sirkap showing the excavated areas, mostly of the 1st centuries BC *and* AD

113

This formidable and Westernizing city was thought by Sir John Marshall to represent the Graeco-Bactrian foundation of the earlier half of the second century BC, albeit that most of the visible remains were ascribed by him to the period when invading Parthians from the north-west assumed control in the first century AD, perhaps shortly after AD 19. Theoretically there was nothing against this. As we now see at Pushkalavati-Shaikhan, it was reasonable to suppose that the Hellenistic grid-system was continued first by the Sakas or Scythians when they arrived in the Punjab early in the first century BC and then by their successors the Parthians in the following century. Both the Scythians and the Parthians were essentially copyists; they retained Greek moneyers and even the Macedonian names for the months, and it may be assumed that their rebuilt Taxila, like their rebuilt Pushkalavati, likewise followed the underlying Greek model.

Nevertheless, during the Scytho-Parthian period at Taxila there was an interesting modification of the town-plan. Along what appears to have been a constant north-south axis it was moved appreciably southwards. In the deep digging carried out by Marshall just inside the northern stone fortification he records seven successive strata. The lowest and oldest was scrappy but was apparently prior to the arrival of the Bactrian Greeks after 180 BC; it seems to have been an outlying vestige of the earliest Taxila which lay mostly three-quarters of a mile away on what is known as the Bhir Mound. The overlying sixth and fifth layers were identified with the Bactrian Greeks, who were the first to occupy the site systematically. The fourth and third layers were thought to represent the so-called Scythians or perhaps a branch of the Yueh-chi who, in some rather ill-defined and perhaps incomplete fashion, had overrun the Bactrian kingdom north of the Hindu Kush about 130 BC, had found their way to the lower Indus valley, and thence deviously reached the Punjab about 80 BC. There about a century later they apparently came in turn under Parthian domination, though the details are far from clear. Of Marshall's two uppermost layers, the earlier is accepted as Parthian whilst the later overlaps the arrival of the Kushan dynasty from Afghanistan and Iran in the second half of the first century AD.

So far so good. This interpretation of the succession of Taxilas over nearly three centuries may well be substantially correct for the northern end of the area demarcated by the surviving stone walls. But the wider significance attributed to his deep digging by Marshall is modified in the light of subsequent excavation carried out in 1944. This was a long and wide trench dug down to the natural soil five hundred and sixty-six yards further south. Here, in the centre of the walled area, there was no sign of the three earliest of Marshall's seven layers. The stratification here began with his fourth layer, dating from the earlier half or middle of the first century BC. Then only – and not, as Marshall thought, by the invading Bactrian

Greeks a century earlier – was the great stone wall, over three miles in length, erected round the city by the Hellenizing Scythians or Scytho-Parthians who now dominated the scene. No doubt, insofar as the new town overlapped its predecessor, the innovators adopted the Greek town-plan, as at Shaikhan. The long main street, for example, slightly side-steps the northern gateway, possibly because this new structure was raised conveniently beside rather than across the inherited axis. But where exactly lay the preceding Greek city and the fortifications which it must certainly have possessed?

Only further digging can establish the answer to these questions, but there is little doubt as to its likely shape. Over five hundred yards to the north of the stone defences are remains of a considerable embankment known as the 'Kacchā Kot' (mud fort), conforming in part with the lines of the adjacent stream (page 103). Superficially this rampart, for such it unmistakably was, is of heaped earth, but scratching at the foot of it has revealed traces of a mud-brick wall, and its original construction may well have resembled that of the defences on the Bordj-i'Abdullah at Begram. Marshall, assuming that the stone defences were Graeco-Bactrian, re-garded this outlying rampart at Taxila-Sirkap as marking 'a well-defined suburb of the city'. This is nonsense. As certainly as can be predicted in advance of excavation, the Kacchā Kot is a vestige of the main fortifica-tion of the Graeco-Bactrian city, which lies partly outside the stone-wall circuit and extends southwards under the northern part of the Scytho-Parthian successor. Its southern limit lies somewhere between Marshall's 'deep digging' and the central trench cut in 1944. At or near its south-western corner a round, flat-topped hill may then have constituted its acropolis. If so, this lost its tactical dominance when the Scytho-Parthian town swept past it up to the summit of the Hathiāl ridge, which com-pletely overshadows it and was doubtless the principal reason for the southward shifting of the city in the Scytho-Parthian period.

Of many buildings outside the fortified area, two are particularly rele-vant to this context. First, some two hundred and fifty yards north of the Kacchā Kot are the restored remains of a remarkable building which was clearly a considerable temple in semi-Classical form (page 116). It is known as Jandiāl, and stands upon an artificial mound in a commanding position overlooking the town. Its overall length is a hundred and fifty-eight feet, and it was constructed of plastered rubble save for the ashlar of the entrances towards the south. The plan is substantially that of a Greek temple with *pronaos* or front porch, *naos* or sanctuary, and *opisthodomos* or back porch. But two features distinguish it from the Classical prototypes: the normal peristyle or surrounding colonnade is replaced by a wall pierced by large windows, and between the sanctuary and the back porch is a solid and deeply founded mass of masonry designed to carry a heavy

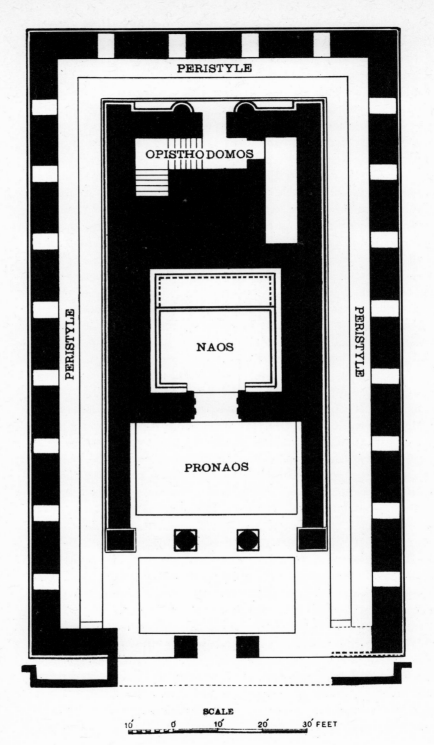

PERISTYLE

PERISTYLE

PERISTYLE

OPISTHODOMOS

NAOS

PRONAOS

SCALE

10'   0'   10'   20'   30' FEET

TAXILA:
*plan of the temple of
Jandiāl, outside Sirkap.
The columns at the
south entrance and at
the adjacent opening
into the* pronaos *were
of the Ionic order*

superstructure and ascended by flights of broad marginal steps. At the outer southern entrance the architrave had been carried across the wide opening by two Ionic columns *in antis*, and a further pair of similar columns and pilasters framed the entrance to the front porch.

For all its generally Classical aspect and its well-carved (though now very fragmentary) Ionic order, this building is unique. No trace of any cult-statue or other apparatus was discovered, and by that token the temple is unlikely to have been Hindu, Buddhist or Jaina. Sir John Marshall's conjecture that the massive platform may have borne a tower some forty feet high in connection with Magian or Zoroastrian worship, either to carry a fire-altar or to enable the worshippers to offer prayers to the sun and moon, holds the field. Indeed, an attribution of this kind would be appropriate to more than one Asian religion of the period. As to the precise date of the Jandiāl temple, no evidence was collected. Marshall speaks of it sometimes as 'erected under the rule of the Bactrian Greeks' (ie *c.* 180–80 BC) and sometimes as belonging to the Scytho-Parthian period of the first centuries BC–AD. Whichever be the more nearly correct, there is at least no doubt that the architect was familiar with Graeco-Bactrian architecture, and that the Ionic capitals and bases were carved by a mason who knew his job. Incidentally, the columns had been built up in proper Classical fashion, with separate drums fixed together with central dowels, and during construction each drum had been ground down by rotation to secure a fine joint.

The second building of special note stood about a mile south-west of Jandiāl, some five hundred yards west of Sirkap and immediately north of the hamlet of Mohra Maliaran. Here, before 1873, a shrine thought to be Buddhist was excavated and produced six columns represented by pedestals, sandstone bases of 'Attic' form and 'several portions of Ionic capitals' of a somewhat rustic kind. One of the capitals, in very weatherworn condition, is preserved with three of the bases in front of the Museum at Lahore (page 118); the date of the building to which they belonged is suggested by the discovery of a foundation-deposit of 'twelve large copper coins of Azes' of the latter half of the first century BC. With the columns from Jandiāl, these are the only examples of the Ionic order at present known, whether in north-western India or in the ancient Bactria, regions where the Corinthian capital is the normal western model.

All this is in context with the Roman or Graeco-Roman objects which Sirkap and its environs have produced in appreciable quantity: glass of the first century AD, a Silenus from the base of a silver bowl and a little bronze Harpocrates, both probably from Alexandria, and stucco sculptures such as a satyr's head and a putto of sufficiently non-Indian, Classical types to indicate a continuing importation of goods and ideas, or even actual artists, from the West (pages 119–120).

TAXILA:
*much-weathered
remains of Ionic
columns found at
Mohra Maliaran,
adjoining Sirkap. Now
in the courtyard of the
Lahore Museum*

I have dallied over certain of the details of these Greek or sub-Greek cities between the western Punjab and the Hindu Kush for two main reasons. First, they have not in some instances been adequately stated hitherto, and the advent of new evidence in recent years has justified or even demanded a general reassessment. And secondly, they demonstrate with astonishing clarity the extent to which the brief transit of Alexander did in fact Hellenize almost instantly vast tracts of Asia populated previously by nomads or semi-nomads and villagers. East of Persepolis and north-eastwards between the Caspian and the Pamirs a miscellany of tribes, which we have loosely identified as Scythians and Parthians, had been penetrated sporadically by the imperial discipline of Achaemenid Persia in the shape of a town or two, such as Cyropolis far up by the great bend of the Jaxartes, and a sprinkling of forts linked by stretches of highway. But all

TAXILA:
*stucco head of a
Graeco-Roman faun
from Sirkap. Height 8½ ins.*
(Taxila Museum)

left
TAXILA:
bust of Silenus or Dionysus from the centre of a silver dish of Graeco-Roman origin. Sirkap, $\frac{1}{1}$

right
TAXILA:
stucco head in Hellenistic or Graeco-Roman style from the Jaulian Monastery. Height $4\frac{1}{2}$ *ins.* (Taxila Museum)

this was policing rather than civilization. The strategy of Alexander, with his Macedonians and Greeks, was also, of course, concerned with the continuing control of the outlands of the old Persian Empire. He too founded his 'Furthest Alexandria' (Chodjend) up by the Jaxartes, with several other cities and military colonies. To that extent he followed and developed the Achaemenid pattern. But there the analogy ceases. The Alexandrian foundations were essentially centres for the planting-out and diffusion of Hellenistic humanism. Their strategic function was pacification by civilization rather then by penalty. Hints at Kandahar and Aï Khanum have already shown something of the cultural completeness of these new centres of Hellenism *in partibus*; of their immediate concern with moral, philosophical, educational and aesthetic problems, essentially Greek but not unaware of an oriental environment.

BEGRAM:
stucco medallion or
emblema *representing*
a helmeted youth
(Ares?). Probably from
Alexandria, 1st century
AD *Diameter* $4\frac{7}{8}$ *ins.*
(Kabul Museum)

And the success of this humane and humanistic policy is demonstrated by the shape of the new towns at which we have glanced – Begram, Pushkalavati-Shaikhan (Charsada), Taxila-Sirkap – built a century and a half after Alexander, but built by Greek or Graecized bearers of the tradition which he had brought to further Asia. And not merely that. When, yet another century later, the Scythians and the Parthians took over, they did so not as destroyers but as understanding heirs to that same tradition. I have already called them copyists and, in a significant sense, that is true. Alexander's humanism had worked; the civilized ideas for which he stood had been adopted by the 'Scythians' and so endured even after the line of the Jaxartes and then that of the Oxus had ceased to contain them. In the East, as in the West, the Greeks conquered by intelligence even when they succumbed politically to force.

No doubt other vestiges of the Indo-Greek period await discovery in the north-western region of Indo-Pakistan, all of them stemming from the adventurings of Alexander, his Greek successors and their Asian pupils. But far away in eastern India, in the state of Orissa, it may also be that a faint vestige of Hellas can still be detected, however unexpectedly, upon the landscape. In the third century BC, and almost certainly as a sequel to the celebrated devastation of the territory of the Kalingas by the young emperor Ashoka in or about the year 261, a four-square town of un-Indian aspect was planted in the vicinity of the medieval and modern Bhubaneswar. The present name of the site is Shishupalgarh, and trial-excavations were carried out there in 1948–9. The enclosure is three-quarters of a mile square, with two entrances set symmetrically in each of the four sides (opposite). The obvious implication, not yet tested by excavation, is that the town was laid out upon an un-Indian grid-plan; and if, as seems likely, it was founded by the emperor Ashoka, whose empire (as we have seen) extended into the Hellenized territories of the north-west, the fair assumption is that it owed something of its rectangularity to the influence of the 'Alexandrias' and their Greek or semi-Greek successors upon that receptive mind. If so, Alexander builded better than he knew.

In summary, then, the latter stages of Alexander's tremendous marches and countermarches from Persepolis to the Punjab left a firm heritage of a Hellenistic kind upon the further East. But that was not the only, nor the most enduring, of the hero's legacies, although perhaps the most personal and positive of them. Alongside, and emerging from, the Greek conquest of the Persian empire a whole chain of eastward reactions was set in motion, which was to have a formative influence upon Indian art, architecture and attitudes until well into the Middle Ages; and in architecture in particular the word 'Persepolitan' was destined to become a cliché amongst historians. To this remarkable sequel to the Alexander saga we may now turn.

opposite
SHISHUPALGARH:
air-view of fortified town near Bhubaneswar, Orissa, mid 3rd century BC. (*North is towards the top*)

UNEMPLOYED
CRAFTSMEN

previous page
PERSEPOLIS:
*lion's head on a double-
ended impost, unused,
for comparison with the
Sarnath lions (opposite)*

SARNATH:
*lions' heads on the
capital of the Ashoka
column, c. 245 BC*

The end of Persepolis was symbolically the end of the Persian empire. In the months which nominally remained to the stricken emperor and his ineffectual substitutes, the empire had no home; to all intents and purposes it had reverted to the nomadism from which, little more than two centuries previously, it had spectacularly emerged.

During those two centuries its achievement, alike in the political and the cultural field, had been remarkable indeed. Politically, though of vagabond origin, it had in some measure unified and disciplined more than three thousand miles of Asia; and, in the absence of inherited skills, it had attuned to its own mentality the contributory skills of a vast miscellany of artists and craftsmen of very various individual extraction. It had created in two hundred years an architecture and a sculpture which would thenceforward take their proper place in the broad history of art as specifically 'Achaemenid Persian'.

Now, with the advent of the Macedonian conqueror, all this had gone up in smoke. Patronage of the Persian kind had vanished overnight and the passage of a hard-bitten army living on its wits – even the wits of an Alexander – was no sort of substitute. The swarming artistry of Persia was, on the instant, out of work. Whither could it turn? Not to the Hellenizing and well-equipped west; there was no useful prospect in that direction. To the north-east? Parthians and Scythians, still essentially in a restless, barbaric village-economy, had nothing to offer. The 'Alexandrias' which the conqueror was strewing in his path, even Justin's legendary 'thousand cities of Bactria', held out no promise; many though not all of them must have been pretty low-grade enterprises, relying for occasional finesse largely upon the alien notions of Greek masters. In one direction only shone a glimmer of hope: along the well-trodden trade-route into India. There city life had been established on an appreciable scale for several centuries. And there, in the years immediately following Alexander's death in 323 BC, events conspired to offer renewed patronage of a kind with which the artists of Persia were familiar. To India accordingly the homeless craftsmen made their way. The official badge of India at the present time, with its stern, addorsed lions, is an ultimate witness to their journeying.

The remarkable circumstances of this cultural migration are reflected alike in history and in monumental evidence, and are an accidental but enduring outcome of Alexander's usurpation of Persia. Briefly, the historical setting was this. When Alexander withdrew from India in 326 on his return-journey to Babylon, he left the territories which he had there overrun as satrapies under the governance of Macedonian officers and Indian rajahs. The details do not here concern us; suffice it that the system quickly broke down, and was not apparently replaced before Alexander's death. New arrangements were made when at Babylon in 323 and at Triparadisus in 321 Alexander's empire was divided amongst his generals and the relevant Asian portion assigned to Seleucus Nicator. But it was not until ten years later that from the tangle of quarrels and intrigues which followed the partition Seleucus was able to turn eastwards, and not perhaps until 305 or 304 that he found an opportunity to confront a sequence of new and dangerous events which now threatened him in north-western India.

There the transit of Alexander had been closely followed by a remarkable upsurge of imperialistic ambition, which no doubt owed its general pattern to the defunct empire of Achaemenid Persia and its immediate stimulus to the recent spectacle of Macedonian imperialism in action. The dual inspiration is easy to understand if we may believe Plutarch's story that as a stripling 'Androcottus', in whom may be recognized the future Mauryan emperor Chandragupta, had seen Alexander himself and had clearly been impressed by the circumstance. 'It is said', adds Plutarch, 'that he often remarked in later times how Alexander came within an ace of making himself master of the country' (ie northern India). At any rate, sometime between 325 and 320 BC this same young Androcottus or Chandragupta, whether thus inspired or not, himself set out with enthusiasm and success upon the path of empire. Again, the circumstances do not matter here in detail but must be summarily recounted.

Briefly what happened was this. Chandragupta, whose surname was Maurya, had served in a soldierly capacity the Nanda king of the little kingdom of Magadha, beside the Ganges in what has more recently been known as South Bihar. Finding himself at odds with his master, he rebelled, failed and was compelled to flee. It seems that he rallied assistance in the Punjab and invaded Magadha from the west; this time he was successful and usurped the throne. In what manner he proceeded to enlarge his petty kingdom is not known; but it is certain that when Seleucus arrived to reclaim Alexander's Indian satrapies he found himself faced by a formidable army under King Chandragupta, and after a tentative engagement ceded to him all the satrapies on the Indian side of the Hindu Kush. Subsequently Chandragupta's son and successor extended his dominions far into the south of India. The kingdom of Magadha had become the Mauryan empire, the greatest empire known by the Indian subcontinent until modern times.

But at first this new empire was a political rather than a cultural unit. There was as yet nothing that could be designated specifically Mauryan art, Mauryan architecture. It was the framework of an empire which lacked cohesive content.

The problem was, in a singular degree, the same that had faced the new Achaemenid empire of Persia over two centuries previously. But this time the answer was at hand. Here under the spreading canopy of the new imperial India was the refuge which the stateless artistry of the dead empire of Susa, Ecbatana, Persepolis was desperately seeking. Here, in the absence of any adequate homegrown tradition, a ready-made patronage awaited hungrily the monumental skills required to embody its religious and secular aspirations on an imperial scale. Indeed the spirit of the young Mauryan empire was willing enough. For two centuries the lands of the middle Ganges, centred upon the kingdom of Magadha, had been in a ferment of ethical and spiritual ideas. There the leaders of Buddhism and Jainism had shaped two of the great moral philosophies of the world: be it repeated that what was lacking was any commensurate material expression. It is worth while to reflect for a moment upon this aesthetic hiatus.

For centuries prior to the advent of the Mauryan empire, the figurative art of India had been essentially a folk-art. It consisted typically of small terracottas representing human or animal forms of a more or less ingenuous character, sometimes expressive and even decorative but partaking rather of nursery or juju than of dignity and sensibility. It was not an adult art in any sense comparable with the growing maturity of Hindu speculation. And as for architecture, in the time of the Buddha there was, so far as we know, little or nothing to which the term 'monumental' can be truthfully applied. The stalwart fortifications which intermittently outlined the vast site of sixth-century Rajgir, in the hills south of Patna, are rough and random masonry, with no hint of refinement. At about the same time, the houses of Hastinapura on the upper Ganges and Kausambi on the lower Jumna were becoming solid and tolerably civilized, but again with no suspicion of architectural sophistication; always with the proviso that the non-survival of domestic timberwork may have impoverished our evidence.

PATALIPUTRA:
Persianizing capital,
c. 3rd century BC
(Patna Museum)

No: it is certain enough that monumental architecture in India begins with the Mauryan dynasty in the years following Alexander, and it begins in a highly significant setting. About the middle of the fifth century BC the capital of Magadha had been transferred from Rajgir to the richer and more accessible plain beside the former junction of the Son and the Ganges, approximately on the site of the present town of Patna. It was here, at Pataliputra, where a border-fortress had been built three-quarters of a century previously, that the usurper Chandragupta Maurya established himself when, as has been related, he seized the kingdom in about 322 BC; and it was hither that some twenty years later Megasthenes came as envoy of Seleucus to the Mauryan court, after the pact between the Greek and Indian kings. Happily, the observant Megasthenes described in some detail what he saw there, and, again happily, intelligible fragments of his writings have come down to us through later writers, notably Strabo (first century BC) and Aelian (third century AD).

He tells us that the city of Pataliputra formed an oblong $9\frac{1}{4}$ miles long and $1\frac{2}{3}$ miles broad, with a defensive ditch two hundred yards wide and a timber palisade with loop-holes for archers; and that the palisade was reinforced by five hundred and seventy towers and pierced by sixty-four gateways. The elongated plan implies that, like the modern Patna, the city stretched almost endlessly along the bank of the Ganges. Its gigantic size, with all allowance for error or exaggeration, indicates that it was the handiwork of the Mauryan emperor himself rather than of his far more humble predecessors, the Nandas. In the royal palace, there was much that 'was calculated to excite admiration, and with which neither Susa, with all its costly splendour, nor Ecbatana, with all its magnificence, can vie. In the parks tame peacocks are kept, and pheasants which have been domesticated; and cultivated plants . . . and shady groves and pastures planted with trees, and tree-branches which the art of the woodman has deftly interwoven. . . . There are also tanks of great beauty in which they keep fish of enormous size but quite tame.' It was, in other words, a Persian 'paradise', and the buildings claimed comparison with those of the Persian kings. There can be no doubt as to whence the general character of Chandragupta's palace was derived. The craftsmen of the old and now defunct Persian empire had found a new and congenial home in the up-rising empire of northern India.

Of the splendour that was Pataliputra little is known to us today in material form, but that little is precisely what the circumstances have already led us to expect. As long ago as 1896 a trial-excavation, conducted without method, brought to light on the site of the Mauryan city a column-capital of a familiar Achaemenian pattern (opposite). It has the stepped impost, side-volutes and central palmettes of its Persian prototypes, and its design if not its execution is attributable to an early phase of the trans-planted Persian craftsmanship. Two stone legs of a throne of Achaemenian type, in the form of winged lions and highly polished in the Persian manner, were also found. Subsequently, in 1912, a more determined attempt was made to reveal the Mauryan city. The methods employed were scarcely more methodical than those of 1896, but the excavator succeeded in un-covering some part of a hall with eighty columns or more upwards of twenty feet high, which may safely be related to the pillared halls of Persepolis (page 132). Fragments of the pillars showed the high polish which in India is distinctive of the Mauryan period and is, as already remarked, of Persian descent, possibly reflecting the polished marbles of Greek Asia. Their wide intercolumniation (fourteen feet) implied a timber superstructure. In front of the columns was a row of massive timber rafts, presumably designed to carry a platform or monumental staircase like those at Persepolis on the unstable subsoil of the site. Renewed excavation hereabouts in 1955–6 produced 'a good number of polished sandstone

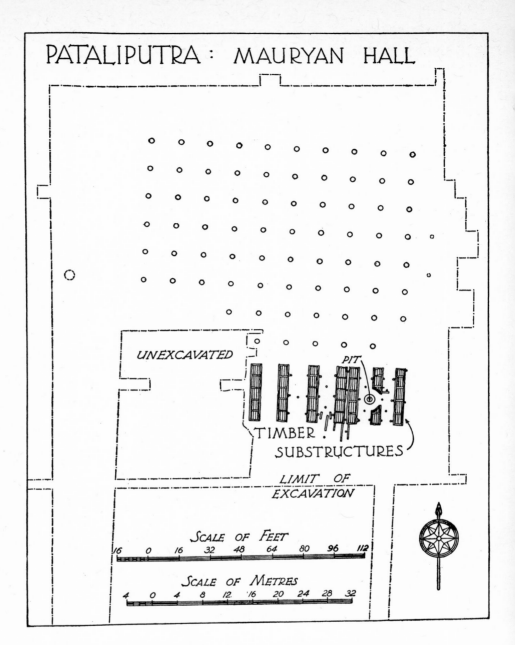

PATALIPUTRA : MAURYAN HALL

UNEXCAVATED

PIT

TIMBER.
SUBSTRUCTURES

LIMIT OF
EXCAVATION

SCALE OF FEET

16 0 16 32 48 64 80 96 112

SCALE OF METRES

4 0 4 8 12 16 20 24 28 32

PATALIPUTRA
*modern Patna: plan of
part of a 3rd-century
hall, recalling those of
Persepolis*

pieces, apparently architectural members, and a mutilated couchant
nandi, the bull of Shiva, found in the same stratum, recalled Mauryan art.
The possibility of the existence of a polished pillar, free-standing or otherwise, seems to be considerable, in view of the discovery of sandstone pieces,
including one six feet by three feet, showing the typical Mauryan polish
and bearing the bead-and-reel pattern and a typically Persian palmette.'

Unsatisfactory though the evidence is in detail, it is clear that we have in the main building a Persian *diwan* or *apadana* or audience-hall, and that we are dealing once more with a deliberate 'Persianization' that bespeaks the presence of imported ideas and doubtless of imported master-masons.

It may be added that the wooden fortification referred to by Megasthenes has also been identified in part by digging (above). A

PATALIPUTRA:
defensive palisade, c. end of 4th century BC

133

double line of upright timbers, fifteen feet high and fourteen-and-a-half feet between the parallel lines, bonded together by a 'floor' and a 'roof' of cross-timbers, has been traced for a considerable distance and appeared to the excavator to 'extend almost indefinitely'. Whether this was a passage within an earthen rampart or whether, as is more likely, the structure was filled with earth and formed its revetment, was not ascertained. This type of fortification is at present without close analogy in India, although Megasthenes records of the Indians that 'all their towns which are down beside the rivers or the sea are made of wood, for towns built of brick would never hold out for any length of time with the rains on the one hand and, on the other, the rivers which rise above their banks. But the towns which are built on elevated places out of reach are made of brick and clay.' It would appear therefore that the fortifications of Pataliputra, unlike the exotic pillared hall, represent an Indian habit. For the rest, the formative influence of the mature craftsmanship of Persia upon the immature experimentalism of India is plain to be seen.

And that influence was by no means limited to the environs of an imperial palace and city. Other illustrations readily present themselves. Take for example the rock-cut religious architecture which from the time of the great Mauryan Ashoka characterized for nearly a thousand years those parts of central India where suitable rock was easily accessible. The earliest datable examples are in the Barabar hills, about forty miles south of Pataliputra. Carved out of the local gneiss, these artificial caves copy timber prototypes, oblong or circular in plan with domed or keel-vaulted roofs and with a glass-like burnish which again recalls the Persian mode. Several inscriptions show that they were dedicated about 250 BC by the Mauryan Ashoka, grandson of Chandragupta, to the use of the Ajivika ascetics, who were rivals of the Buddhists and the Jainas. In view of the adherence of Ashoka to the Buddhist persuasion, the dedication is a tribute to the reality of the tolerance which the emperor so often preached in his numerous inscriptions – some of them, as we have seen, as far away as Kandahar.

Here the important point is that these rock-cut 'structures' (and many more of later dates) are not of a kind native to pre-Mauryan India. Their generic prototypes are to be recognized in the tombs which, in the likeness of pillared halls, had been cut into the cliffs of Media and Persia from the seventh century BC or earlier (page 29). Ashoka now adopted the Perso-Median concept whilst adapting it to the Indian idiom and usage. The Barabar cave-buildings – the earliest rock-cut 'structures' in India – retain the Persian polish of the stone but represent with close verisimilitude local structures of timber and thatch. One of them, the Lomas Rishi cave, is an oblong vaulted hall entered by a pseudo-timber doorway of Indian pattern carved and sculptured with great precision and skill. Another, the Sudama, is a barrel-vaulted hall enclosing at its inner end a circular 'thatched' hut or shrine with walls of simulated vertical planking, again with the astonishingly mirror-like polish. Later rock-cut halls are of a more ambitiously architectural character. But throughout we are presented with a recurrent quality of the Indian mind: its aptitude to borrow and at the same time to transmute.

Whilst we consider the rock-cut architecture which is doubtless a true link between Mauryan India and Achaemenid Persia, there is another aspect of Indian building which recalls Persia, though with less certain affinity. Underlying resemblances of form or concept there is of course the fundamental factor that both the Persian and the Indian architects were attacking similar problems with the same materials and under similar conditions. Both were thinking largely in terms of timber and mud-brick. Both were liable to use rock or masonry as a more permanent medium in which to render the forms that timber had suggested to them. True, they were both accomplished masons within the simple compass of trabeate construction, the only engineering problem being that of supporting a vertical weight of greater or less degree, with negligible lateral thrust. But in neither case was there normally any real integral relationship between the individual stones of the structure and its architectural or sculptural design. It may therefore be that a further technological similarity between them, to which reference has already been made, is no more than accidental. It is this. 'The Median stone-masons,' observes Herzfeld, 'when making columns, windows or stairs, used to build up an artificial rock of the size and approximate shape required, and carved the wanted object out of that rock, as a sculptor carves a figure out of the raw block. Never is the object dissected into its structural components, in order to shape the stones according to their function. Old Iranian masonry never gets far away from the origin, the fashioning of rocks.' In Greek masonry, he adds, 'the function rules the shape. Such a thing has never been attempted in Iranian masonry.' It so happens, whether causatively or not, that the same thing is essentially true of Indian masonry. Far down into the Middle Ages it remained a practice to build an Indian temple of rough blocks and to carve them into architectural and sculptural shape afterwards. (I illustrate a medieval example from Orissa (pages 136–7), but the tradition goes far back.) The only appreciable difference between the rock-cut and the freebuilt structure was the physical act in the latter case of quarrying and transporting the stones, and the necessity for providing an outside as well as an inside for the building. It may be added that in Indian architecture the resulting detachment of carver from builder was liable to lead, at the best, to a riotous and challenging independence of the decorative element and, at the worst, to the treatment of the building as a mere poster-hoarding or postage-stamp album. By reason of its essentially static and architectural quality Persian

overleaf
MAHENDRAGIRI
*district Ganjam,
Orissa: unfinished
medieval temple*

overleaf opposite
MAHENDRAGIRI:
completed temple

135

sculpture offended less flamboyantly in this respect, but even there the solemn processions of gods and tyrants, soldiery and tribute-bearers are in great measure (unless repetitively climbing a staircase) unconscious of the vagaries of the building which they adorn.

But there remain other practices of Mauryan and later India which are indisputable inheritances of the Persian tradition. In a previous chapter instances have been cited of Ashoka's employment of wayside rocks and architecture for the dissemination of moral and social exhortation (page 65). Once more it is easy to detect Persian precedent in an Indian environment. The Bisutun or Behistun rock-inscription of Darius I in western Persia dates from *c.* 518 BC; there is in India no precursor to the rock-edicts cut at the bidding of Ashoka in and after 257 BC. It is true that, save for an occasional formula which further links the two series, nothing could be more unlike the commemorative and administrative records of the proud Persian despots than the gentle though firm admonishments of the Buddhist emperor. Yet again we are confronted with the transmutation of a manifestly borrowed idea.

More than one of these Persianizing trends are displayed by the famous sandstone columns, once over thirty in number, which Ashoka set up presumably after his conversion to Buddhism. At first their sculptural symbolism sufficed to indicate their purpose, but on some of them the emperor later amplified and particularized his message by adding inscriptions conveying pious exhortations such as those which he had already advertized in the Rock Edicts. By that time, if not earlier, the columns were explicitly integrated with the Buddhist profession of faith and morality. It is just possible that they originally had a less specialized connotation. The erection of independent pillars was certainly a native, not an imported, habit. In the classical West, monumental columns are not known before the Roman empire, unless indeed we include the evidences of pillar-worship in Minoan Crete or the famous column which was carved between guardian lions over the gateway of Mycenae in or about the thirteenth century BC. (The significance of that column has never been convincingly discovered.) But in India the use of the wooden memorial pillar is of equally early, if not earlier date. As the *yūpa*, commemorating some special sacrifice, it abounds already in the Vedic literature. Or it might be the memorial of a great victory; its significance no doubt varied. In Indian cosmology the shaft tended to represent the cosmic axis between heaven and earth. An ancient and persistent legend relates that each day 'from the depths of a lake in the Himalayan fastnesses there rises a great shaft supporting a throne that towers up to support the sun in the zenith, and with the setting of the orb sinks again into the depths'. At the four sides of the lake were figures in the shape of a lion, a horse, a bull and an elephant, indicating the four cardinal points of the compass. All this is echoed in the most elaborate of all the

SARNATH:
*capital of the Ashoka
column, c. 245 BC.*
(Sarnath Museum)

139

Ashokan pillar-capitals, that at Sarnath and now the official badge of India, on which four steadfast Persian-looking lions, once rendered sterner by inlay within the now-empty eye-sockets, royally supported the sun-disc symbolizing cosmic law above a circular abacus carved with the four animals between subsidiary discs (page 139). Whether in origin specifically Buddhist or not, the central ideas of the Ashokan pillars were through and through Indian.

But at the same time the whole expression, architectural and sculptural, of these stone pillars is derivative. If nothing quite like them is known before the third century BC – and then only in Mauryan India – the elements composing them are nevertheless indubitably Achaemenid Persian. The shafts all show the high Persian mirror-like polish to which reference has already been made. They lack the fluting of the columns of Persepolis, but other Persian columns, as at Pasargadae, are unfluted. They taper skywards with an average diameter of three feet, and are more than forty feet in height, without base but with the addition of a bell-shaped or lotus capital which recalls this element in the capitals of Persepolis. Above the capital, a circular abacus carries the sacred symbol or symbols – one or other of the four cosmic animals or, as we have seen at Sarnath, the four addorsed lions formerly bearing the sacred wheel of golden bronze. And on the Sarnath capital the lions at least go straight back to Achaemenid Persia and then to eighth- and seventh-century Assyria. (Good Assyrian examples are to be found amongst the splendid ivory-carvings found by Professor M. E. L. Mallowan at Nimrud by the Tigris.) Nor did the wanderings of these royal beasts cease there. Far to the West, they are at home in the Classical art of the eastern Mediterranean, and in passing we have already observed them on the Homeric lion-gate at Mycenae. Throughout this wide expanse they display a basic uniformity tempered by local idiosyncrasy.

And there is another thing about these lions. Unlike their highly naturalistic predecessors in the Assyrian lion-hunts, or the equally convincing horses, bulls and elephants with which they alternated or associated in the Buddhist complex, they have a peculiarly heraldic and fabulous quality which sets them apart from the world of everyday. This differentiation is mainly due, no doubt, to the conventional status of the lion as an established emblem of kingship or authority; the Buddha was himself described as 'the Lion of the Sakya Clan'. An archaic and symbolic lion-concept had become sanctified by long and hieratic usage, and so discouraged representational deviation. But in an idle moment a contributory reason has presented itself to my thoughts. Horses, bulls and elephants were all familiar domestic animals, all of them models complaisantly ready to the artist's eye. Not so the lion. True, there were lions then in many regions where they are nowadays rare or absent. (In the Indian subcontinent the hundred or

SARNATH:
*Persianizing Indian
capital, c. 2nd century
BC.* (Sarnath
Museum)

two lions which still lurk in a limited area of the west represent a former lion-population of more respectable size.) But whether rare or abundant, the lion presents one difficulty to his delineator: he is not a convenient or passive model! Torn by the alternatives of personal discomfiture or adherence to a pictographic convention, the artist's choice was not in doubt. Anyway, for one reason or another, the heraldic lion persisted.

But even on the Sarnath column-capital, for all its close affinity with Persian modes, there are traces of the local (Indian) idiosyncrasy to which I have referred. Here, and elsewhere amongst the Mauryan sculptures, can be detected a softening of the muscular forms that may be ascribed to the Indian pupil rather than to the Persian master. This trend is more clearly manifest in another column-capital from Sarnath (above); it bears the Persian volutes, but the horseman on one side and the elephant on the other are unmistakably Indian. It may be as late as the second century BC. On the other hand the comparable capital from Pataliputra, with volutes and palmettes and bead-and-reel, is nearer to the Persian prototype and is probably not later than the third century (page 130). And a similar dating in the early Mauryan period may be ascribed to the polished sandstone fragment already mentioned, which was likewise carved with bead-and-reel and palmette and was found in a low level on the same site in 1955. Here Hellenistic analogues suggest themselves almost as readily as Persian, though no doubt the immediate source is in fact Achaemenian.

Column-capitals. I have just been turning over again the pages of a standard history of Indian architecture, and from the third century BC until far into the Middle Ages I find the word 'Persepolitan' used recurrently to describe the column-capitals of free-built or rock-cut Indian shrines. It would not be too much to say that the bell- or lotus-element which the Persians had adapted for their own columns from the Egyptian West now became the basic character of the first known Indian order of architecture, however varied or Indianized from time to time and place to place. Let it be repeated that prior to the aftermath of Persepolis there was, so far as we know in the absence of timber survivals, nothing in India that could be truly called an evolved architectural style: and let it be also repeated that, having taken root with a dramatic historical suddenness, this transplanted mode of Persia flourished and endured as, in a much later age and a more devious fashion, the sub-classical amalgam of the Renaissance endured long and flourished variously in western Europe.

This is a notable fact and deserves representative illustration. In the absence of closely dated architecture from Pataliputra, which was a burgeoning metropolis before 300 BC, the earliest known Indian adaptations of the Persian architectural tradition are the monumental Ashokan columns of which something has been said. A century later, and less than two centuries after Alexander, the Persian elements which his advent had displaced were firmly and widely incorporated in Indian architecture. In the latter part of the second century BC (perhaps as late as 100) a close and well-known simulacrum of the Ashoka columns was dedicated to Vasudeva (Krishna) at Besnagar in central India, by the Indianizing Greek Heliodorus, who had come as an envoy of Antialcidas, the Greek or Greek-named king of Taxila. Not merely is the Persian lotus-capital faithfully repeated but, for the first known occasion in India as it seems, the shaft is partly fluted and partly facetted in reminiscence of the fluted Persepolitan model. There are many later examples of this feature in India, and the absence of earlier ones is no doubt accidental.

To the same period belongs, on inscriptional evidence, the surviving gateway (now in the Indian Museum, Calcutta) from the eastern side of the famous stupa or shrine at Bharhut near Nagod, also in central India. It is flanked by two pillars, each consisting of four clustered and facetted shafts crowned by Persepolitan capitals which combine to carry two pairs of animals, one of lions and one of human-headed bulls. Ultimate Assyrian influence may here be detected, but the intermediary was again Persia, and the large honeysuckle motif on the massive *acroterion* which surmounts the gate emphasises this Graeco-Achaemenian link. Consistently the masons' marks are in the Kharoṣthī alphabet, which was derived from the Aramaic alphabet of Achaemenid Persia and was characteristic of the borderlands of north-western India in and after Ashokan times.

This use of animals on the impost of a column-capital is an important feature of the Persian inheritance in India; its adoption by the Indian architects and sculptors points alike to the durability of the alien inspiration and to the imaginative adaptability of the Indian recipient. In Persia the weight of the architrave-beam was commonly transmitted through an impost-block or bracket, spread laterally to take the beam and thus unlike the normal square impost of the more classical orders of the West (page 40). There was a tendency to carve the ends of these oblong impost-blocks into animal-forms, thus producing the 'protomes' or double animals, back to back, which are well illustrated at Persepolis and occur widely in the lands of the Persian empire. An evolved Indian version, from many which might be chosen, can be seen in the rock-cut *chaitya* or temple-hall at Karli,

opposite
KARLI
western India:
colonnade of Buddhist
prayer-hall, c. 1st
century BC, *showing*
vestiges of the
'Persepolitan' capital

south-east of Bombay, dating probably from the end of the first century BC (page 143). There the bell-shaped capitals, coarsened descendants of the 'Persepolitan' type but now associated with Indian bases (vase-shaped but possibly derived from Achaemenid bolster-bases such as have been noted at Aï Khanum), are surmounted by imposts bearing at their ends admirably carved animals (elephants or horses) in place of the 'protomes'. They carry bejewelled male and female figures, and all is now Indian save the initial formula. Incidentally, in front of this *chaitya* and others like it were two rather crude columns carrying bell-capitals crowned by lions in fading but recognizable Ashokan fashion.

The centuries passed but the 'Persepolitan' capital continued. Near Delhi at the Qtub Mosque, but brought anciently from elsewhere, stands the famous iron pillar set up, as an inscription upon it tells us, in memory of a mighty king named Chandra who may have been Chandragupta II (AD 375–413) of the imperial Gupta dynasty (opposite). It was a standard to the honour of the Hindu god Vishnu and probably bore at one time a figure of the bird-man 'vehicle' of Vishnu on its summit. The parentage of the bell- or lotus-capital is still unmistakable. Incidentally, the almost rustless iron of the pillar is a well-known technical marvel; the nearest analogues are large iron 'beams' at the famous thirteenth-century temple of Konarak in eastern India, possibly from the same region.

And so the story could go on. At Sanchi in central India, in the fifth century AD, and at Badami in western India, in the sixth, the 'Persepolitan' capital survives recognizably, with spreading impost though with all manner of elaboration. But the inherited Persian 'order' was now being increasingly overwhelmed and transmuted by the infinite fertility of the Indian mind, true child of its own exuberant jungles. After something like a thousand years – not a negligible afterlife! – the fertile ashes of Persepolis had at last ceased in any appreciable degree to fertilize. It is a tempting but idle thought to wonder what might have been if Alexander had fallen to his wounds at the Issus in 333 BC. It is likely enough that much of the cultural expression of a whole sub-continent for a millennium or more would have taken a significantly different shape, and much that is familiar and agreeable in Indian architecture would never have come into being.

opposite
QTUB MOSQUE:
iron pillar, c. AD 400, at the Qtub Mosque near Delhi, showing the persistence of the 'Persepolitan' tradition

GANDHARA

The last two chapters have carried the aftermath of Persepolis into the Indian Middle Ages and beyond. From the official badge of modern India and from the rock-cut shrines and the principal architectural 'order' of the medieval subcontinent the paths have led backwards to the *diaspora* of Persian craftsmanship after 330 BC and to the substitution a few years later of the Mauryan empire of the Ganges as a source of patronage for that of the Achaemenids. These were amongst the immediate and substantive sequels to the transit of Alexander, all of them strangely wide of the conqueror's intent. His shade, in search of some familiar fulfilment of his thinking, must have been the unhappiest of spectres. In fact, only the trim Hellenizing towns which Alexander and his successors imposed here and there upon the alien landscapes of Bactria and northern India may be thought to have offered for a while some shadowy consolation. Nevertheless these towns, in the light of recent discovery, have given a new impetus to a much-discussed problem of art-history which stems partially from the Greek tradition and is now well worthy of fresh argument.

The problem is this. In the latter half of the nineteenth century the north-west frontier of India, the ancient Gandhara, began to yield to European curiosity innumerable fragments of a remarkable art to which the name Gandharan has long been comprehensively applied. Vast quantities of stone sculpture, normally reliefs cut in green schist from the environs of the Peshawar plain, were supplemented by mass-produced stucco sculptures, mostly if not wholly relating to the Mahayana Buddhism which flourished in the region during the early centuries AD. Precise dating for this complex manifestation is not even yet available. In spite of recent and ambitious probing in the prolific region of Swat and a better controlled but slighter contact in Afghanistan, it is still unhappily true to say that not a single productive Gandharan Buddhist site has been excavated with an adequate regard to modern analytical method. It can, however, be affirmed that no true example of Gandharan art has been found in a stratigraphical context earlier than the establishment of the Kushan dynasty in India, sometime in the latter part of the first century AD; and broadly the period AD 100–450 is probably not very far wrong for the school as a whole, if we exclude the possibility of immature or experimental works at a slightly earlier period. The terminal date, by which time schist had been largely superseded by stucco and clay, is given by the savage invasions of the White Huns or Ephthalites, who broke in from central Asia in the latter half of the fifth century. Thereafter the art may have lingered or revived in odd corners but was for the most part blotted out in the holocaust. The Hun king is credited by the Chinese traveller Hiuen Tsang, who visited the region about AD 630, with the extermination of the royal family of Gandhara, the slaughter of more than 90,000 of the population, and the destruction of 1,600 Buddhist monasteries. It is scarcely surprising that when he died 'the air was darkened and the earth quaked and fierce winds rushed forth as he went down to the Hell of unceasing torment'.

Now this frontier art, in spite of a general uniformity of content and a profound unity of purpose, was in fact a highly complicated amalgam. In the earlier days of its modern recognition, nostalgic Western expatriates who collected it abundantly from the soils and bazaars of the busy frontier region attuned it uncritically to their predominantly Classical education and found it full of Greek or Graeco-Roman reminiscence. As an alternative to 'Gandharan' the term 'Graeco-Buddhist' or even 'Graeco-Scythian' was loosely applied to the whole amalgam; and the standing and sheeted Buddha himself was likened to the Socrates and other togate worthies of the Hellenistic or Graeco-Roman tradition. Kilted Classical figures, an occasional 'Athena' or an 'Atlas' and, not least, the recurring framework of Corinthian columns and pilasters fitted into the picture of a far-flung provincial outpost of the familiar Mediterranean world. Here was something that was easily understood by Victorian soldiers and civil servants, whose descendants to the present day cling to fragmentary Buddhas or Bodhisattvas in the dwindling cabinets and attics of the English scene.

Before we attempt to analyse this art a little more closely, let it be admitted at once that the Classical, Graeco-Roman element in it is authentic enough. Beyond doubt, the Greek or Graeco-Roman West had a hand

in its iconography, if not in its actual manufacture. Examples will be cited presently. But first let it also be accepted that the Western element is subordinate to others of very different origin, that it is in fact a minority component in the art as a whole. If the repetitive Corinthian pillars and pilasters be set aside, the Classical traits, whilst readily recognizable, are far less emphatic than European critics have been inclined to pretend. The Gandharan Buddha himself, save in the transient role of ascetic, is essentially a plump Hindu princeling, and his robe, however reminiscent superficially of a Classical himation or toga, is equally at home in the world of Hindustan as a normal monastic garb. Usually the figures which environ him or enact the stories of his previous births are similarly Indian; and alien variations more frequently reflect the modes and moods of inner Asia than of the Western Classical periphery.

Nevertheless, this art remains alluringly composite and eclectic. Indian, Iranian, Graeco-Roman – those are its principal constituents in variable proportion. We are here concerned mainly with the last of these under the stimulus of the new evidence from Alexander's Bactria; but before we focus upon this lively problem, the three major components may usefully be defined, with brief illustration.

First, the Indian element. This aspect of Gandharan art is basic. The art was contrived to meet the needs of the wealthy Buddhist communities of the regions on both sides of the modern Pakistan-Afghan border, and that was its primary home; though its influence eventually extended far afield, into central Asia on the one hand and into southern India on the other. Geographically it was in its early maturity the occupant of the region, extending from the Oxus to the widespread Indus system, which had been politically Graeco-Bactrian and Indo-Greek. But the cult upon which it subsisted – and without which it is unlikely to have been born – was through and through, spiritually and socially, Hindu. However much it ultimately flourished in the mountainous frontier-lands, it was basically

GANDHARA ART: *stair-riser showing Corinthian half-columns and six 'donors' in a free style displaying Western influence. Possibly 2nd century* AD. (Peshawar Museum)

GANDHARA ART:
*relief found near
Yakubi in the Swabi
sub-division of the
Peshawar district,
showing the preaching
Buddha on a lotus
throne. At the top left is
a Buddha in meditation
within an arched
shrine supported by a
'Persepolitan' column;
below left is a
Bodhisattva under an
Indian trefoil arch on
Corinthian columns.*
(Peshawar Museum)

a product of the plains and jungles of the middle Ganges. If Gandharan art were stripped of all contemporary alien elements, it would still survive in some shape as an *Indian* art. The relief opposite will suffice here as an example. Its small Corinthian and Persepolitan pillars do not obscure its inherently Indian quality.

Secondly, there is the Iranian or Parthian element, manifest notably in the occurrence of Iranian or Parthian costume on certain Gandharan reliefs (see above). The importance of this phenomenon, however, should not be over-emphasized. Trousered Iranians such as appear on certain of the Gandharan reliefs must have been widely familiar in the mixed Irano-Kushan society of the borderland wherein the sculptors worked, but do not of themselves necessarily imply any very significant intrusion of Iranian artistry. Indeed, perhaps the finest example of such imagery – the well-known frieze, probably of donors, now in the Gandharan collection of the Museum of Archaeology at Toronto – has been cited plausibly in a contrary sense. The frieze, which terminates in a little statuesque Eros standing in a niche, shows six elegantly bearded and curled noblemen, in trousered Iranian dress and armed with massive Kushana swords, in a variety of free though courtly attitudes (page 148). But a competent critic is more impressed stylistically by their Classical affinities. 'They stand', observes Soper, 'with the nonchalant ease of figures on a Roman frieze; ... they are as different as possible from the stiffly frontal, identically rendered Kushan lords at Mathura. I am tempted to believe that the idea of rendering a row of donors in this way was suggested by a cartoon from the Imperial workshop, presenting the Muses as a roughly similar problem of figure-spacing.' In this comment there is an element of subjectivity, but there is at least a case for considering here whether we have not in fact a mode borrowed from the Classical tradition to illustrate an Iranian (or Kushan) scene, doubtless in a Buddhist setting. Gandharan reliefs in a comparable 'illusionist' manner will be cited below.

Other Iranian or Parthian figures from Gandhara do indeed come nearer to a Parthian style, though still far from the hard, precise,

153

linear modes of Palmyra and Hatra. A relief from Shotorak, a Buddhist site fifty miles north of Kabul in Afghanistan, shows a trousered Parthian or Iranian standing beside a woman with Classical costume and hair-style; exactly the sort of juxtaposition that would be in place at Palmyra or Dura within the Parthian zone. A stone figure, now at Peshawar, from Sahri Bahlol on the Peshawar plain displays beaded decoration on the trousers and a kuftan or coat in the Iranian fashion, and the decorated belt has analogies at Hatra. But, inspite of the recorded caravan and sea traffic from Palmyra to India, there is singularly little in Gandharan sculpture that points indubitably to the western fringe of Parthia. The occasional 'frontality' in the Gandharan complex (see below) is advanced in this context but is not necessarily Parthian. True, the habit of presenting gods and indeed lesser folk stolidly staring outwards at the spectator occurs at semi-Parthian Palmyra at least as early as the first century AD; and Rostovtzeff, who, from his vantage-point at Dura on the Euphrates has been described as the founder of the study of Parthian art, recognized the trait in the handi-work of 'Iranian nomads' (Scythians and Sarmatians) in South Russia as far back as the third century BC. Further, he claimed that 'it was certainly the Sakians [Scythians] who taught the principle of frontality to the artists and artisans of Gandhara'.

This, it must be confessed, is a doubtful saying. 'Frontality' has more than a single root. It is deeply implanted in the basic soil of most unevolved

GANDHARA ART: *relief from the Dharmarajika Stupa, Taxila, showing the Buddha in benediction, accompanied by his bearded associate Vajrapani with thunderbolt and surrounded by a family of women and children. The group illustrates Gandharan 'frontality'.* (National Museum, Karachi)

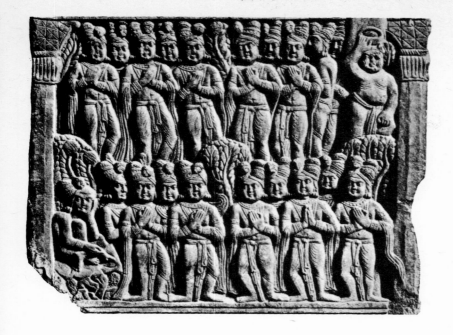

BHARHUT
*Central India:
example of 'frontality'
on a Buddhist pillar,
2nd century* BC

aesthetic; it is a part of the simple generalized concept of child-art the world over. It occurs in archaic Greek art. It is liable to be rationalized and formalized in societies prone to servility in their confrontation with gods and potentates, though the Achaemenian Persians escaped it and adhered to profiles. It may become a habitual and accepted artistic convention in an otherwise developed aesthetic; as when the sculptors of the Severan reliefs (*c.* AD 203) at Lepcis Magna in Tripolitania, under Asian influence, represent both the royal family and the surrounding crowd with steadfast frontal gaze. But Gandharan art, let it be repeated, was primarily an Indian art in the service of a Hindu creed. And the principle of frontality had already been admitted to Indian art in the second century BC. At Bharhut in central India the famous Buddhist reliefs of that period (see above) show serried ranks of outwardly facing acolytes in what might be regarded as a type-specimen of frontality; incidentally with the tiered 'perspective' which likewise recurs often enough in Gandharan as indeed in developed Roman Imperial art.

In short, features such as these appear widely and intermittently in Asian art, and there form an underlying continuum which, in any particular time or place, may be either more or less emphatic. The Westernizing bias of Achaemenian Persia suppressed them; the recrudescent Iranian tendencies – if they must be so-called – of post-Achaemenian art accepted them. The Śunga art of India in the second century BC was within the range of the continuum, and in due course contributed to the formation of the Gandhara complex. There is no need to travel laboriously to Mesopotamia or South Russia for the fountain-source.

Thirdly, we return to the Western or Classical element. And first let us resume for a moment the question raised above by the Toronto relief of Iranian noblemen and its allegedly Roman affinities. In similar fashion other Gandharan stone friezes have been regarded as significantly Western in manner; three are illustrated on pages 151, above and 158. That on this page, a well-known example at Calcutta, shows an undivided sequence of episodes in the Buddha's life in a manner somewhat recalling the 'continuous style' which appeared on the one hand at Pergamon in Asia Minor as early as 180 BC, and on the other hand at Bharhut in central India in the latter half of the same century; its primary source, if it has a single origin, cannot be identified. The Calcutta relief represents the home-coming of the Buddha after his Enlightenment, and the sequence of incidents begins with the story of the dog who barked on the entry of the Buddha and in the sequel was revealed, with surprising inconsequence, as the reincarnation of the host's father. But the notable aspect of these friezes is their style: the figures move freely and naturally in a great variety of poses, in what is known commonly to art-historians as an 'illusionist' manner. They *breathe* and *move*. I quote A. C. Soper: 'I know only one part of the Western world in the century of Kushan magnificence [the second century AD] that produced an art comparable to the Gandharan sculpture analysed above: the west Mediterranean area centring on Rome. In the frieze-sarcophagi that made up the bulk of the Roman sculptural output of the second century, there is the same manipulation of the human figure . . . , the same delight in producing the illusion of a stage peopled by living actors.' The critic goes on to recall the recorded contacts between the 'Bactrian' régime and Rome during the earlier second century: the account in the *Historia Augusta* of the emperor Hadrian's conciliatory attitude towards the Eastern powers, when 'the "Bactrian kings" [who-ever they may then have been] sent to him envoys as suppliants for his friendship'; and when, in the 'Epitome of the Caesars', the 'Indians, Bactrians and Hyrcanians' respectfully sent envoys to Antoninus Pius. Soper suggests that one such mission secured at Rome the services of a master sculptor, who was escorted back to Peshawar 'to lend a properly imperial note to the rapidly expanding art of Gandhara'. And in the same vein another critic, Benjamin Rowland, bravely affirms that 'it was unquestionably the introduction of bands of foreign workmen from the eastern centres of the Roman Empire that led to the creation of the first Buddhist sculptures in the Peshawar Valley'.

This view may well be a part of the story, however difficult of proof. The importation of Western craftsmen into Gandhara is a likely enough postulate. Greeks or professed Greeks or at any rate Westerners were familiar figures in many parts of India. The oft-quoted story of the purchase of St Thomas in Syria as a skilled craftsman on behalf of King Gondophares of Taxila (about AD 40) goes back to the third-century *Apocryphal Acts of the Apostles* and must at least have been sufficiently likely to gain credence. But, apart from this, Greeks as 'Ionians' under one or other of the variant names Yonaka (Sanskrit), Yona (Prakrit), or more usually Yavana (Sanskrit) are mentioned abundantly from the second century BC onwards; and the last name, which retains at its centre the sound of the long-obsolete Greek digamma ('Ιᾱϝων) and is comparable with the parallel Hebrew Javan or Yawan, must represent an ancient borrowing, no doubt (as is generally supposed) through early Achaemenid Persia. We sometimes overlook the astonishingly cosmopolitan free-for-all of the ancient Eurasian world.

And the Greek or Graeco-Roman impact upon Gandharan art is by no means restricted to debatable elements of style. I like to quote a direct and indisputable confrontation between West and East (see below): a stone relief now preserved in a private collection in England but said, with all likelihood, to have come from ancient Pushkalavati (the modern Charsada)

GANDHARA ART: *stone relief probably from Charsada, showing Laocoön probing the Trojan horse. A mixture of classical figures, with an Indian Cassandra emerging from a gate of Troy on the left*

157

on the Peshawar plain. It shows the unmistakable wooden horse of Troy in the hands of suspicious Trojans, one of whom, no doubt the Laocoön of Vergil's *Aeneid* II, 233 ff., prods it with a spear. The heroes are in approximately Classical dress, but on the left a very Indian Cassandra, bare to the waist, emerges from a gate of Troy, vociferously prophesying her unheard forebodings. Whether the scene was designed literally to represent the Trojan episode or whether, as has been suggested, it was here adapted to some unidentified Buddhist folk-tale, there can be no doubt as to its iconographic origin. It is the Vergilian scene, carved by an Indo-Greek (or Indo-Roman) sculptor.

Then again there are those little Corinthian columns and pilasters which were introduced habitually by the Gandhara carvers into otherwise Indian contexts. Where did they come from and how? Their companions, the columns with 'Persepolitan' capitals and bases, are another matter which, in a previous chapter, has presented us with no great difficulty; and now the Corinthian motifs too are beginning at last to fit more happily into the picture. Their natural and rational source would be in accessible Hellenistic architecture; and Aï Khanum has shown us, as a sample, where to look for it. Moreover, thanks to Daniel Schlumberger's recent and monumental excavation of the imperial Kushan shrine at Surkh Kotal in the middle of Afghanistan – a shrine dated by inscription (page 166) to the great Kanishka I, sometime in the earlier part of the second century AD – we can see these Corinthian pilasters, already in their sub-Hellenistic structural and sculptural guise, at an intermediate stage in their actual transit from Greek Bactria to Gandhara. At Surkh Kotal they occur both in the temple-complex itself and upon the Buddhist platform which was built seemingly somewhat later on the lower ground a mile away. But, as Schlumberger points out, there is nothing that can be described either as Buddhist or as Indian in the shrine itself and its immediate environs. The

colonnaded portico in which the shrine stands is a Classical rather than a Persian or Buddhist feature. Ornamental details are Western; such as a frieze of garlands carried by Erotes, as also found in Gandharan carving at Taxila and elsewhere but Graeco-Roman in origin (see below). True, the temple itself is Persian, and so are the stepped merlons from the surround (compare Susa and Persepolis). The whole 'climate' of the place may be summed up as Graeco- or Romano-Iranian. There is no detail that in any sense proclaims an Indian source; and the inference which I have borrowed from Schlumberger, that here we have formative elements of Bactrian and Persian art and architecture on their way to Gandhara and to inclusion in the Gandharan amalgam, is an attractive one. Incidentally, it is of interest to note that the Corinthian columns and pilasters never penetrated beyond Gandhara and the Punjab. In the further depths of the Kushan Empire, for instance in metropolitan Mathura south of Delhi, they may be looked for in vain.

In one way and another, then, the venerable problem of Gandharan art, its affinities and origins, is at last beginning to assume a rational shape. At one end of the story stands the creative genius of Alexander the Great; at the other end, as it seems, the splendid opportunism of the greatest of the Kushans, Kanishka 1; and between the two a busy four centuries of political movement and cultural interchange.

To recapitulate with some slight historical amplification. Let it again be emphasised that the Gandharan art is rooted in the region covered previously by the Greek province and kingdom in Bactria, roughly between the Hindu Kush and the Oxus, with its extension into India as far as the Indus and its tributaries. That extension began momentarily in the time of Alexander the Great in 326 BC, but was enlarged by enterprising and dissident Bactrian Greeks somewhere about 180 BC. The Bactrian kingdom itself was overrun by semi-nomadic tribesmen from the region of the Jaxartes at

opposite, top
Tetradrachm of Menander, c. 150 BC, *obverse.* Enlarged 2/1. (British Museum)

opposite, bottom
Tetradrachm of Menander, reverse. Pallas Athene hurling thunderbolt. Greek inscription: 'Of Menander, King and Saviour'

GANDHARA ART:
relief from the Kunala Monastery, Taxila, showing putti *or* amorini *with a looped garland. Behind are a winged woman and a man and woman in three-quarter view. The garland motif recurs in Gandhara art and is derived from Graeco-Roman prototypes.* (National Museum, Karachi)

a date conventionally estimated at about 130 BC, leaving the Indo-Greek kingdom south of the Hindu Kush as the only surviving independent Greek outlier in this part of Asia. There it endured until about 80 BC, when in turn it was taken on the flank by the spreading Scythians.

To this summary statement, however, recent work has added a new possibility of importance in the present context. The tribesmen, whoever they were, who conquered Bactria within a few years of 130 BC may not in fact have blotted out the Greek urban life which they found there. I understand from Monsieur Bernard, the excavator of the Greek city at Aï Khanum (above, pages 75ff.), that he suspects a continuance of Greek city life there, in however reduced a form, after 130 BC. The place seems to have ended in flames, followed after an interval by an earthquake which was succeeded in turn by widespread pillaging for metal cramps and building-material; but the essential date, that of the burning, awaits the results of further excavation. It may well be that appreciable parts of the city remained upstanding long after the semi-nomadic tribesmen of the Oxus-Jaxartes-Atrek region arrived upon the scene. And these tribesmen were no fools. Whether Scythians or Parthians or some branch or other of the Yueh-chi, they had for long enough been in intermittent contact with Persian and Macedonian (Hellenistic) civilization in the form of cities or military colonies to appreciate something of its value. When they reached Gandhara and the Punjab in the course of the two following centuries, at Charsada (Pushkalavati) and Taxila and presumably elsewhere they continued to build on Greek foundations, and this process culminated in the highly civilized empire of the Kushans, themselves a sept of the central Asian Yueh-chi. It were easy to picture these invaders from the borders of China and the rough-and-tumble deserts or mountains of central Asia as forerunners of the bloodthirsty hordes of a Mihirakula, a Timur or a Genghis Khan, but to do so would be to mislead. Over the years they came ultimately to conquer but also to learn, and it may well be that from the outset they tolerated and profited from habitable Graeco-Bactrian cities as they certainly tolerated or re-used the Indo-Greek cities in their turn.

And, not least, their entry into India brought them into contact with a religious philosophy not out of keeping with the Zoroastrianism to which some of them had adhered during their passage through Iran. It was in the Indo-Greek kingdom, centring upon the Gandharan frontier-zone and the Punjab, with vacillating frontiers which may ultimately have included Mathura south of Delhi and Broach on the west coast, that the Buddhism which was to become the firm base of Gandharan art burgeoned in pre-Kushan days. As we have seen, already in the middle of the third century BC the Buddhist precepts wherewith Ashoka bound his very miscellaneous empire were proclaimed as far afield as Kandahar which, if not in Indo-

Graecia, lay close beyond its borders. At some unknown date or dates, three of the four great stupas which commemorated the Buddha's bodily charity were located in Gandhara and the Punjab: those of the Body-gift at Manikyala (Punjab), the Flesh-gift between Peshawar and Buner, and the Eye-gift shortly north of Pushkalavati. As Tarn puts it, the region became to Buddhists a veritable Holy Land. And it seems probable that these Buddhist trends, which with the catholicity of the Hindu mind never excluded other cults and creeds, were nevertheless confirmed in a substantially Buddhist dominance in the time of the famous Menander, greatest of the Indo-Greek kings, who ruled the region from about 160 to 140 BC or a trifle later. (The terminal dates are arguable but the argument is of little consequence.) Menander's sensitive visage is recorded abundantly upon his coinage; nowhere more intelligently and convincingly than on a fine silver tetradrachm recently acquired by the British Museum (page 160). It is rather that of a pope or a poet than of the successful general of obscure origin which indeed he was. It is authentically that of the king who governed with a council of Greeks or Yonakas (five hundred is the conventional and no doubt highly inflated number recorded); who, if not a Buddhist in any official or corporate sense, stood very near to Buddhism and traditionally received honours after death which reflect those of the Buddha himself; who inspired a remarkable and still extant work of disputation of an almost Platonic kind, the *Milindepanha* or *Questions of Milinda*, a name which is an accepted transcription of Menander; and who, alone of all Alexander's successors, became a legend, a historical king who transcended the bounds of history. This ultimate honour was not attained by Ashoka himself, and it cast an imperishable fascination over the land which Menander 'King and Saviour' governed and the cult wherewith, in some intangible sense, he was associated.

Now during the two centuries after Menander's death fresh developments became manifest in the Buddhist cult. What had begun as a moral philosophy culminating in the blessed state of negation, with the Buddha as the prophet and archetype of enlightenment, now partook increasingly of the character of a religion centred upon the Buddha as a spiritual presence, as indeed a god. Whereas previously it had been as sternly improper to represent the prophet of Buddhism in material form as it still is to represent the prophet of Islam, it was now no less fitting to represent the deified Buddha than to embody the traditional divinities of the Hindu pantheon. Simultaneously, the Bodhisattvas, from being merely former incarnations of the Buddha and vague forces of charity and mercy, now became the saintly colleagues or apostles of the divine Buddha in his spiritual mission to lead all living beings to perfection. Aesthetically, the change was of high importance; it created a possibility and a demand for a new, evolved iconography, in some sense parallel with the possibilities and demands of

the new Christianity which was at the same time taking shape in the West. Here was one of those recurrent moments when a large part of the civilized world was simultaneously in spiritual and intellectual ferment, and seeking new formulae in which to express this adventurous unease.

But where in India were this new iconography and its fabricators to come from? In particular, how was the north-western zone, which had been Indo-Greek and had subsequently continued very much on its traditional way under Scythian and Parthian overlords, to satisfy the new and demanding needs of its Buddhist majority? For this much at least seems certain: unlike the Jumna and Ganges valleys and central India, where there were considerable existing schools of sculpture, there was at this time in the north-west no established art worthy of the name upon which to draw in this unprecedented situation. As the evidence stands, neither at Taxila (Sirkap) nor at Pushkalavati (Shaikhan) is there any substantial evidence of native artistic output appreciably above the folk-level (left). We can now, with more confidence than hitherto, postulate dusty vestiges of Graeco-Bactrian art here and there in more or less derelict Hellenistic cities, but the fire had gone out of it. Terracotta (rarely stone) toys and votive objects, yes, sometimes with a recognizably classical trend remained in production, and occasional trade-objects of some slight aesthetic consequence; but nothing capable of expressing a rich, growing and complex faith such as the new Mahayana Buddhism. In the future home of Gandharan art there was essentially a vacuum.

And then the answer came, with all the might and majesty and fire of a great and vital revelation. It came from the north-west of the Hindu Kush, from the modern Afghanistan, the ancient Bactria and its environs. Led by a sturdy nobility armed with massive broadswords, clad in flowing kuftans and billowing trousers gathered at the ankle about redoubtable boots proof against the sandy and stony paths of inner Asia, the Kushans swept into the ancient kingdom of Menander and, at some disputed date after the middle of the first century AD, began the consolidation of the great Kushan empire in India. They brought with them wealth and energy; they brought, too, a knowledge of the surviving traditions of Iran, and they knew something of the dying – but perhaps not even yet quite dead – Greek cities of Bactria. And now to the south-east of the mountains they found orderly cities, less cultivated than those of Bactria but still of a substantially Greek kind, upon which their own receptive minds were not slow in getting to work.

We have seen a little of their handiwork. Capable of fighting and of paying their way, the new rulers recruited artists and craftsmen from far and wide: from the great river valleys of the northern plains, from the Iranian territories whence they themselves had come, from the lingering cities of Greek Bactria with their Corinthian colonnades and their fading Hellenistic sculptures, such as Paul Bernard has begun to show us from

Aï Khanum; and perhaps too from the Romanizing regions of western Asia. The work of Alexander and his successors began to live again in a new environment, with new stimulus and with new collaboration. At the same time, trade flourished, and poured luxury goods from the ends of the earth into the storerooms of Begram, beneath the Hindu Kush: glassware and bronzes and stucco *emblemata* from Alexandria in Egypt (pages 121, 159, 168, 170–1), priceless ivories from Mathura, lacquer bowls from China. It is likely enough that trade in goods was supplemented by trade in craftsmen. In such a multitude of ways the composite art of Gandhara was brought into being by the Kushans and, above all, by their great emperor Kanishka 1 at the beginning of the second century AD. The dates of Kanishka's reign are a classic problem of Indian history; there is evidence which may indicate that he was on the throne about AD 128. It is more important that we have a tolerable picture of the man himself and of his widely ranging mind. His statue at Mathura (page 165) unhappily lacks the vigorous bearded head, which we can reconstruct in the mind's eye from his coins (page 149). But the kuftan, the vast riding-boots defiantly out-turned, the scabbarded broadsword firmly gripped, and the massive club bespeak the man. His imperial shrine at Surkh Kotal, with its great inscription, shows in monumental form the script which his Kushans had adapted, no doubt in Bactria, from Hellenistic sources (see above). His gold currency, on the accepted Roman standard (if not actually Roman coinage re-used), bears stamped upon it a strange eclectic assortment of Eastern and Western deities, with a Roman emperor for good measure. Here was an Eastern monarch, an Eastern mind, with a roving curiosity and powerful enterprise, suited above all to be the patron of a vigorous eclectic art: an art established quite suddenly, almost tumultuously, in a vacuum; an *Ersatz* art, an *Esperanto* art, contrived from widely disparate sources, but an art, which served its purpose of mass-communication and so was multiplied almost beyond belief.

But to isolate the sources and tributaries of an art, or some of them, is a long way short of an appraisal of its combined status. Apart from its interest as a superabundant historical improvisation and as a still incompletely solved problem in time, what is its place as a serious and major contribution to the history of art? Answer to a question of this sort need not be disqualified by its subjectivity.

I have just described Gandharan art as an art of mass-communication. Indeed, one of the first characters of Gandharan art is its astonishing proliferation. Even now its fragments are not very difficult to acquire by the reasonably knowledgeable seeker. Those who have opportunity to see and handle it in quantity may indeed begin to suffer a sense of satiety after a while, in spite of diversities of subject, skill, material and cultural affinity. If, in spite of these relieving qualities, the eye is not to weary a trifle of so much over-all uniformity of purpose, so much repetitive earnestness rarely enlivened by moments of secular release (see below), it is perhaps helpful to recall the dual purpose of this art.

On the one hand it was devotional and instructive. If its Buddha, standing statuesquely or seated in meditation and instruction, is as repetitive as are our own endless statues of the Madonna or of Christ, the analogy contains the answer. If vast surfaces of stone, stucco or clay are covered with figures, often of a rustic kind but occasionally of considerable quality, enacting a hundred Buddhist stories and folk-tales, the Western

GANDHARA ART: *stone base with two leonine feet, between which two partially dressed women entertain two men. The scene is of a type common enough in Western Classical art.* (Lahore Museum)

left
BEGRAM:
Roman cut-glass vessel
from the great hoard,
1st–2nd century AD.
(Kabul Museum)

right
BEGRAM:
Roman glass vessel from
the great hoard,
1st–2nd century AD.
(Kabul Museum)

mind may properly reflect upon the religious paintings which at one time covered the walls and bejewelled the windows of our Christian churches with didactic scenes from the scriptures, depicted with a wide range of artistry and often with bucolic undertones. Be it repeated that all this, in East and West alike, was mass-communication in a not very literate age, and the parallel is sufficiently exact.

On the other hand there runs through Buddhist as through Christian art the linked vanity and aspiration of the donor. Tireless repetitions of the Buddha and of the *jatakas* or life-stories of the Buddha and the Bodhisattvas gratified the pride of countless donors and helped them to attract the interest of the divine philosopher in the required direction. Perhaps unhappily, this sort of reiteration was gradually aided and cheapened by the increasing use of painted stucco, until in the latter stages, for example, of the monasteries around Taxila stucco sculpture scarcely fell short of mechanical mass-production. In this form, Saint-Sulpice had indeed come to Gandhara and the Punjab, and was thence finding its way up the mountain paths towards eastern Asia. It is a chastening thought for a Westerner that the use of facile stucco almost certainly reached the East along the well-worn trade-routes from Egyptian Alexandria which, with its enormous natural supplies of the raw material, must take some responsibility for its broadcast dispersal. Reference may be made to illustrations on pages 119, 120 and 121.

In passing judgment, then, upon this frontier art we may (in resumé) properly regard these factors: *first*, that the region was marked by a dominantly Buddhist faith, long established hereabouts but now increasingly iconic and ritualistic in its expression; *secondly*, it was a region which was nevertheless flanked on the one side by the surviving vestiges of the Graeco-Bactrian art and architecture that may now be confidently assumed, and on the other by the established artistry of inner India; a region, *thirdly*, which had no traditional art of its own appreciably above the folk-level; and *fourthly* a region which was now (at the end of the first century AD) settled by strong and intelligent invaders with an international outlook and a quick understanding of the deeply religious (and therefore political) needs of this broad and difficult frontier-region, lying across major international trade-routes and vital to the growth and security of the new Kushana empire. A later empire sought ineffectually to settle this great border-problem by means of a multitude of forts and alien soldiers. Kanishka and his Kushans actually settled it – by a multitude of monasteries garrisoned by thousands of home-grown Buddhist monks.

These factors combine, I think, to explain much of the quality of Gandhara art. It acquired the deep roots of a folk-art, but it was trimmed and cherished by all manner of imported expertise. It was, within its manifest limits, a success. It was at the same time a popular and a specialist art. Where, as occasionally, it breaks away momentarily from the narrower confines of its special mission, an intrusion of the Graeco-Roman ethos may sometimes be detected, reflecting the essential secularity of all Greek thinking (page 167).

Finally, before we leave the Gandharan Problem, a word as to previous theories regarding its composition and origin. The earlier conjectures were based upon the assumption that Gandharan art was essentially the straight combination of Classical Greek and oriental elements in the service of Gandharan Buddhism, and the sobriquet Graeco-Buddhist was commonly applied to it. The Greek component was traced uncritically to the Greek province established by Alexander in Bactria, afterwards promoted unilaterally to the Greek kingdom of Bactria. In 1889 Vincent Smith affirmed that both in time and in character the Western Classical aspects more nearly equated with Roman than with Greek times and prototypes, and proposed the name Romano-Buddhist as a substitute for Graeco-Buddhist. How the Roman elements reached Gandhara was not fully explained.

In and after 1905, A. Foucher, to whom Gandharan studies are greatly indebted, came a trifle deviously to the conclusion that the direct link between Bactria and Gandhara would not work. He pointed out (correctly, as the evidence then stood), that Greek Bactria, whilst it had left us a superb Hellenistic coinage, had not bequeathed a vestige of Greek architecture, sculpture or painting. Moreover, Greek Bactria had been blotted out by nomads about 130 BC. In any case the supposed existence of a Graeco-Bactrian school was a mere myth. When the Greek Bactrians fled across the

BEGRAM:
one of several Graeco-
Roman bronze bowls
from the great hoard.
1st–2nd century AD.
(Kabul Museum)

Hindu Kush into Gandhara and beyond, the Buddhists of the region were not yet either numerous or strong enough to build, or stimulate the building of, a new Buddhist civilization. It was not until nearly the end of the second century AD that they were ready; and then it was in Gandhara itself that Gandharan art appeared, something like three centuries after Greek Bactria had come to an end. But it was also more than two centuries since the derivative Indo-Greek régime in Gandhara had been superseded, and north-western India was now ruled by invaders (the Kushans) who had no concern either with Greek civilization or with Buddhism. Therefore the origins of the Indo-Greek art of Gandhara could not in fact be later than the end of the Indo-Greek régime, about 80 BC.

All this somewhat tangled and even contradictory argument summarizes half a century of theorising by a somewhat abstract scholar with little evidence at his disposal. In an attempt to bring it down to earth, some years ago I was bold enough to revive Vincent Smith's insistence upon the Roman affinities of Gandharan art in the light of the remarkable discoveries of Roman trade-objects at Begram and elsewhere dating from the first and second centuries AD. Here, it seemed, was a possible and indeed documented link between East and West during the formative period of the art. There is, I think, still something in this theory in an ancillary sense, and it points, as I believe significantly, to close and important if intermittent relations between East and West in the Roman Imperial period. But it is by no means the whole explanation of our problem.

And then in 1960 Daniel Schlumberger entered upon the scene with two important articles in the periodical *Syria*. He asserted bluntly that a significant Graeco-Bactrian art, parental to that of Gandhara, was not a myth; it had simply not been discovered. He was right. His inspiration was derived from his then-current excavation on the remarkable Kushan site

at Surkh Kotal, and the recognition there of Classical and Persian elements but nothing specifically Indian. The site therefore exhibited the sort of artistic equipment which the Kushans brought with them on their south-easterly migrations, after long contacts with Iranian peoples and places further north and at least a passing acquaintance with substantial if dwindling (or even dead) Greek cities in Bactria and beyond. And now Aï Khanum is on the point of proving this supposition. We can now, since 1965, affirm that the Kushans must have ridden down Hellenistic streets lined with dusty Corinthian colonnades, and have seen Hellenistic statuary, some of it still standing in its proper environment. Even if, as now seems unlikely, Aï Khanum and other cities of the kind perished suddenly in 130 BC, something of their grandeur must have survived to attract and instruct the intelligent Kushan wanderers, even as they camped awhile amongst their upstanding ruins.

Aï Khanum and Surkh Kotal between them have thus significantly changed the aspect of the Gandharan problem; not, be it emphasized, as a brand-new catalyst but as confirmation of contributory elements which have hitherto been little more than a guess. So too those third-century Greek inscriptions from Kandahar; new witnesses to a living and sophisticated expatriate Greek society in intelligent liaison with oriental thought, and consistent with that move towards a non-Greek or neo-Greek internationalism which Tarn liked to see in the receptive genius of Alexander.

In these pages I have sought to assemble the new facts and old theories into something like an organic unit. And in doing so I am conscious that the whole story, touching upon far-reaching revolutions in thinking and expression, in urban life, in the arts and in craftsmanship, goes back to the circumstance that Alexander the Great, against the hopes of some of his followers, turned east and not west after that turbulent party at Persepolis.

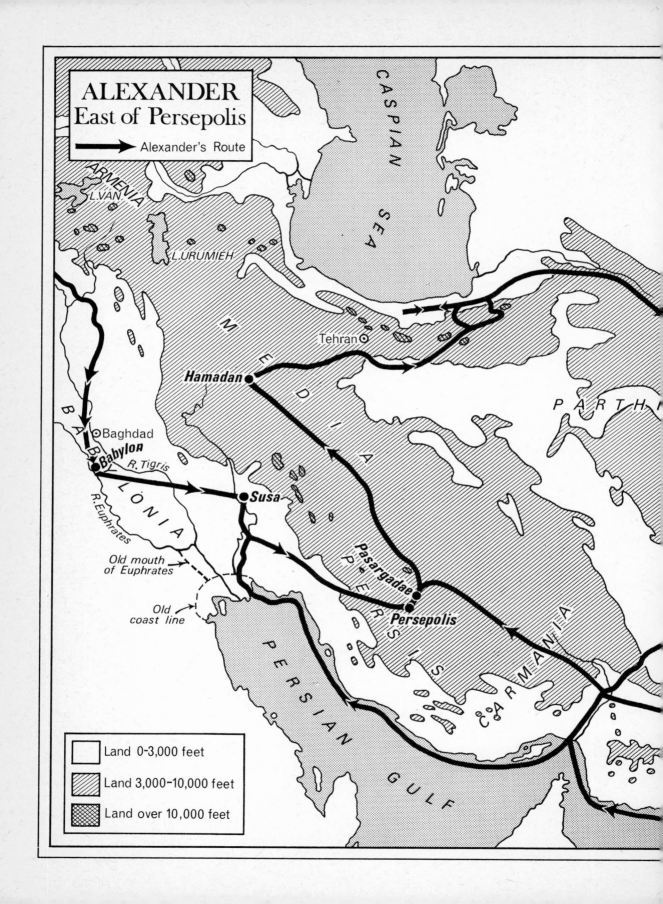

ALEXANDER
East of Persepolis

→ Alexander's Route

ARMENIA
L.VAN
L.URUMIEH

CASPIAN SEA

M E D I A

Tehran ⊙

Hamadan

PARTHI

Baghdad
Babylon
R.Tigris

B A B Y L O N I A

R.Euphrates

Old mouth
of Euphrates

Old
coast line

Susa

Pasargadae

P E R S I S

Persepolis

CARMANIA

PERSIAN GULF

Land 0-3,000 feet

Land 3,000-10,000 feet

Land over 10,000 feet

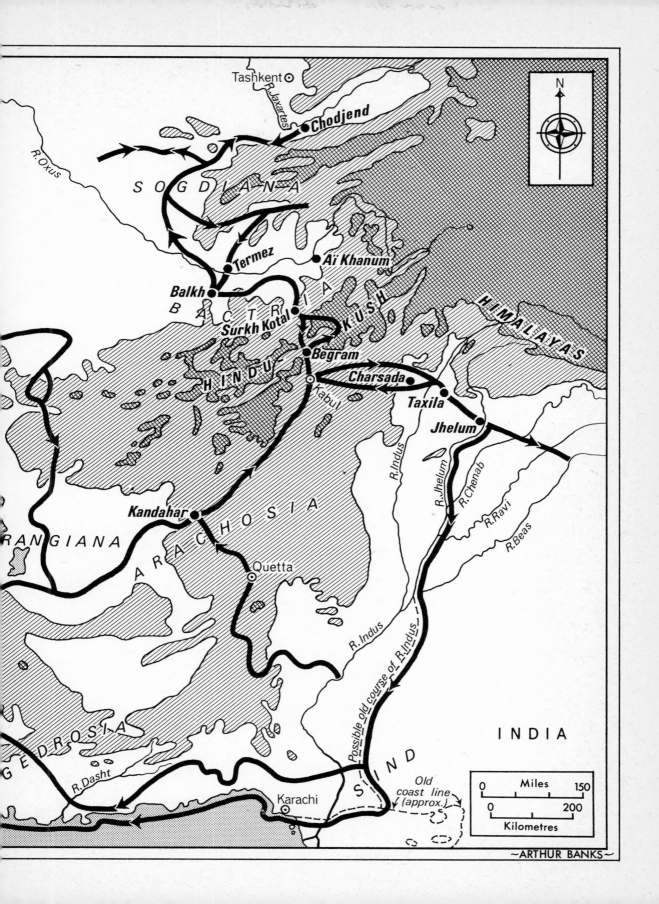

Tashkent ⊙

R.Jaxartes

Chodjend

SOGDIANA

R.Oxus

Termez

Aï Khanum

Balkh

B   C T R I A

Surkh Kotal

HINDU —   KUSH

HIMALAYAS

Begram

Charsada

Taxila

Kabul

Jhelum

R.Indus

R.Jhelum

R.Chenab

R.Ravi

R.Beas

Kandahar

A R A C H O S I A

Quetta

RANGIANA

R.Indus

GEDROSIA

Possible old course of R.Indus

R.Dasht

S I N D

Karachi

Old coast line (approx.)

INDIA

	Miles	
0		150
0		200
	Kilometres	

~ARTHUR BANKS~

NOTES

This is not a book for which an infinitude of footnotes is an apt harassment, but a few bulk references and recent additions (sometimes not easy of access) may justly be demanded.

Foremost are the monumental works of W. W. Tarn: *Alexander the Great*, i. Narrative, ii. Sources and Studies (Cambridge University Press, 1948); and *The Greeks in Bactria and India* (2nd edition, Cambridge University Press, 1951).

These massive and ingenious treatises of Tarn's will remain essential sourcebooks for all students in the foreseeable future. This is not to say that they are infallible in judgment or free from wilful prejudice, and the author's rudimentary understanding of archaeology is itself far out-dated. On more than one occasion in the preceding pages it has been found necessary to question or discard his views, but only after careful and appreciative examination of them.

A useful collection of sixteen miscellaneous excerpts from English, American, German, Austrian and Swiss publications is *Alexander the Great, the Main Problems*, edited by G. T. Griffith (Heffer, Cambridge, 1966). It includes, in particular, W. W. Tarn's British Academy lecture on 'Alexander and the Unity of Mankind', with E. Badian's commentary.

The Cambridge History of India: i (1922) is naturally out of date but, as a solid work of historical scholarship, has a permanent value if read critically.

FOREWORD

For the heraldry of the Nine Worthies in the fifteenth century see:
F. J. Furnivall, 'The Nine Worthies and the Heraldic Arms they bore', in *Notes and Queries*, 7th S., viii (London, 1889), 22. This note relates to Harleian ms.2259 in the British Museum, and in particular to folio 39 verso. Dr C. E. Wright, of the Department of Manuscripts, tells me that this ms. is known to heraldic students as the 'Strangways Book', a treatise on arms written in the 1450s by Richard Strangways of the Inner Temple. See Hugh Stanford London, 'Medieval Treatises on English Heraldry', *The Antiquaries Journal*, xxxiii (London, 1953), 174–182

THE BURNING

Arrian, *Anabasis*, trans. as *The Life of Alexander the Great*, by Aubrey de Selincourt (The Penguin Classics, 1958). Passim, but particularly iii, 18 ff.
Diodorus Siculus, Library of History, xvii 69–73. Encounter with the suppliant Greeks; the capture and destruction of Persepolis; the death of Darius iii. Trans. by C. Bradford Welles. (Loeb Classical Library, Diodorus viii, 1963)
Plutarch, *Lives:* Alexander. Ed. by B. Perrin. (Loeb Classical Library, Plutarch vii, 1918, reprinted 1949)
W. W. Tarn, *Alexander the Great*, ii, Sources and Studies, esp. pp. 47–49 on Thaïs, and pp. 127–133 on Cleitarchus
Frank Adcock, 'W. W. Tarn', obituary in *Proc. of the British Academy*, xliv (London, 1958), 253–262

D. Stronach, 'Excavations at Pasargadae',
in *Iran* I–III (London, 1963–5, British Insti-
tute of Persian Studies, c/o The British
Academy, Burlington Gardens, London, W1)
Erich F. Schmidt, *Persepolis*, I, Structures,
Reliefs, Inscriptions (University of Chicago
Press, 1953)
E. Herzfeld, *Iran in the Ancient East* (London
and New York, 1941)
Gisela M. A. Richter, 'Greeks in Persia',
American Journal of Archaeology, I (1946),
15–30. Esp. for the Greek graffiti on the foot
of Darius I

THE BACKGROUND OF THE BURNING

For Achaemenian art see:
Henri Frankfort, *The Art and Architecture of
the Ancient Orient* (The Pelican History of
Art, 1954), pp. 202–233
Also, Frankfort, 'Achaemenian Sculpture',
in *American Journal of Archaeology*, I (1946),
6–14
Gisela M. A. Richter, 'Greeks in Persia', as
cited above
Also, see E. F. Schmidt as cited above

AFTER THE BURNING: I

For the two important Greek inscriptions
found at Kandahar, Afghanistan, in 1958
and 1963 see:
Daniel Schlumberger, Louis Robert, André
Dupont-Sommer, and Émile Benveniste,
'Une bilingue gréco-araméenne d'Asoka', in
Journal Asiatique, 1958 (Paris), pp. 1–48
Daniel Schlumberger, 'Une nouvelle in-
scription grecque d'Açoka', *Académie des In-
scriptions et Belles-Lettres*, 22 mai 1964
For the newly discovered and partially
excavated city at Aï Khanum, beside the
Oxus in Bactria, see interim reports:
Daniel Schlumberger, 'Aï Khanoum, une
ville hellénistique en Afghanistan', *Académie
des Inscriptions et Belles-Lettres*, janvier-juin,
1965
Daniel Schlumberger and Paul Bernard,
'Aï Khanoum', in *Bulletin de Correspondance
Hellénique*, LXXXIX, 1965, ii, pp. 590–657
Paul Bernard, 'Deuxième campagne de
fouilles d'Aï Kanoum en Bactriane,' *Académie des Inscriptions et Belles-Lettres*, avril-juin,
1967
Paul Bernard, 'Aï Khanoum', in *Proceedings
of the British Academy*, LIII (London, 1968)

For the city of Begram, see:
R. Ghirsham, *Bégram, recherches archéologiques
et historiques sur les Kouchans*, 'Mémoires de
l'Institut Français d'Archéologie Orientale
du Caire', tome LXXIX, and 'Mém. de la
Délégation Arch. Fr. en Afghanistan', tome
XII (Cairo, 1946)

For the great hoard of Roman, Indian and
Chinese objects found at Begram in 1937
and 1939, see:
J. Hackin, *Recherches archéologiques à Bégram*,
'Mém. de la Délégation Arch. Fr. en Af-
ghanistan', tome IX (Paris, 1939)
J. Hackin and others, *Nouvelles recherches
archéologiques à Bégram*, 'Mém. de la Déllég.
Arch. Fr. en Afghanistan', tome XI (Paris,
1954)
Mortimer Wheeler, *Rome beyond the Imperial
Frontiers* (London, 1954), chapter XIII

For Pushkalavati, former capital of Gandhara, near the modern Charsada, see:
Mortimer Wheeler, *Charsada, a Metropolis of
the North-West Frontier* (Oxford, 1962)
A. H. Dani, 'Shaikhan Dheri Excavation',
Ancient Pakistan II (Peshawar University,
1967)

For Taxila, in Pakistan, see:
John Marshall, *Taxila* (Cambridge, 1951)
Also *A Guide to Taxila*, 4th ed. (Cambridge,
1960)

UNEMPLOYED CRAFTSMAN

For the migration of craftsmen and ideas
from the defunct Achaemenian empire of
Persia to the new Mauryan empire of India,
see:
A. U. Pope, 'Some interrelations between
Persian and Indian architecture', in *Indian
Art and Letters*, new series, IX (1935), pp.
101 ff.
R. E. M. Wheeler, 'Iran and India in pre-
Islamic times', in *Ancient India*, no. 4 (Archae-
ological Survey of India, New Delhi, 1948),
pp. 94–103. See this reference for the
Mauryan palace at Pataliputra
Percy Brown, *Indian Architecture (Buddhist and
Hindu)*, (Bombay, 1942 and 1946), chapters
III and IV
Benjamin Rowland, 'The World's Image in
Indian Architecture', in *Journal of the Royal*

Society of Arts, 1964 (London) for a discussion of Buddhist symbols

For 'Persepolitan' capitals, see Benjamin Rowland and R.E.M.Wheeler as cited above

For the Bharhut architecture and carvings, see:
N.G.Majumdar, *A Guide to the Sculptures in the Indian Museum at Calcutta* (Delhi, 1937)

GANDHARA

For Gandhara and related arts, the most valuable discussion in recent years, with special reference to origins, is by Daniel Schlumberger, 'Descendants non-Méditerranéens de l'art grec', in *Syria* XXXVII (Paris, 1960), 131–166 and 252–318. This considers Kushan art in relation to Iran and Greek Bactria which, even prior to the discovery of Aï Khanum (see notes on page 175), he regarded as a primary source. His essay, stimulated by his own excavation of the Kushana dynastic shrine at Surkh Kotal in central Afghanistan, has perhaps an excessive *préoccupation grecque* but is full of ideas. For a preliminary summary of Surkh Kotal, see Schlumberger, 'The Excavations at Surkh Kotal and the Problem of Hellenism in Bactria', in *Proceedings of the British Academy*, XLVII (London, 1961), 77–95

For a summary of the position of the Gandhara controversy in 1963, see M.Wheeler, 'Gandhara Art: a note on the Present Position', in *Le Rayonnement des civilisations grecques et romaines sur les cultures périphériques* (8me Congrès International d'Archéologie Classique, Paris, 1963)

For earlier views on Gandhara art, see A. Foucher, *L'Art gréco-bouddhique de Gandhara* (Paris: I, 1905; II, 1, 1918; II, 2, 1922; II, 3, 1951); and *La Vieille Route de l'Inde de Bactres à Taxila*, Mémoires de la Délégation Française en Afghanistan (Paris; I, 1942; II, 1947) See also:
L.Bachhofer, 'On Greeks and Śakas in India', in *Journal of the American Oriental Society*, LXI (1941), pp. 223 ff.
H.Buchthal, 'The Western Aspects of Gandhara Sculpture', in *Proceedings of the British Academy*, XXXI (London, 1948)
R.E.M.Wheeler, 'Romano-Buddhist Art: an Old Problem Restated', in *Antiquity* XXIII (1949), 4–19; and *Rome Beyond the Imperial Frontiers* (London, 1955), pp. 167–171
A.C.Soper, 'The Roman Style in Gandhara', in *American Journal of Archaeology*, 55 (1951), 301–319
Benjamin Rowland, *The Art and Architecture of India* (Penguin Books, 1953), pp. 79 ff.
Islay Lyons and Harald Ingholt, *Gandharan Art in Pakistan* (Pantheon Books, New York, 1957). An excellent album of photographs, with commentary
J.Meunié, *Shotorak*, Mémoires de la Délégation Française en Afghanistan (Paris, 1942)

For Parthian and other related art, see:
M.I.Rostovtzeff, 'Dura and the Problem of Parthian Art', in *Yale Classical Studies*, ed. by A.M.Harmon, V (New Haven, 1935), 155–304
M.Rostovtzeff, *Dura-Europos and its Art* (Oxford, 1938)
J.B.Ward-Perkins, 'The Roman West and the Parthian East', in *Proceedings of the British Academy*, LI (London, 1966), 175–200

For recent views as to the dating of Kanishka I, with special reference to the evidence of Surkh Kotal, see:
A.D.H.Bivar, 'The Kanishka dating from Surkh Kotal', *Bulletin of the School of Oriental and African Studies*, vol. XXVI, part 3 (University of London, 1963), 498–502
R.Göbl, 'Die drei Versionen der Kanishka-Inschrift von Surkh Kotal', *Österreichische Akademie der Wissenschaften, Philosophische-historische Klasse Denkschriften*, 88 Band, 1 Abhandlung (Vienna, 1965)

For Kushana art see:
John M.Rosenfield, *The Dynastic Arts of the Kushans* (University of California Press, 1967)

ILLUSTRATIONS

Thanks are due to the Archaeological Survey of India, the Archaeological Department of Pakistan, the Indian Museum at Calcutta, the Government Museum at Peshawar, the Museum at Lahore, the Museum of Archaeology at Toronto, and the British Museum for the courtesy of supplying photographs. Professor A. H. Dani, of Peshawar University, readily placed at the author's disposal the results of his important excavations at Charsada-Shaikhan; and both Mr Daniel Schlumberger and his successor as Director of the Délégation Archéologique Française en Afghanistan, Mr Paul Bernard, have shown extreme courtesy and liberality in supplying information and photographs relating to the Greek inscriptions from Kandahar and, above all, the dramatic discovery and excavation of the Hellenistic city at Aï Khanum.

INDEX

DATE DUE			
NOV 2 1 2006			
			PRINTED IN U.S.A.
GAYLORD